Database Modeling
Step-by-Step

T0174093

Database Modeling Step-by-Step

Gavin Powell

CRC Press
Taylor & Francis Group
Boca Raton London New York

CRC Press is an imprint of the
Taylor & Francis Group, an **informa** business

Taylor & Francis Group
6000 Broken Sound Parkway NW, Suite 300
Boca Raton, FL 33487-2742

© 2020 by Gavin Powell
CRC Press is an imprint of Taylor & Francis Group, an Informa business

No claim to original U.S. Government works

Printed on acid-free paper

International Standard Book Number-13: 978-0-367-42217-2 (Hardback)

Visit the Taylor & Francis Web site at
http://www.taylorandfrancis.com

and the CRC Press Web site at

Trademarks Used in This Publication

Contents

Contents   vii

List of Figures   xi

Preface   xvii

About the Author   xix

Chapter 1   The Evolution of Relational Database Modeling   1

1.1   From File Systems to Object-Relational Databases   2

    1.1.1   File Systems   3

    1.1.2   The Hierarchical Database Model   3

    1.1.3   The Network Database Model   4

    1.1.4   The Relational Database Model   5

    1.1.5   The Object Database Model   7

    1.1.6   The Object-Relational Database Model   9

1.2   General Types of Database Models   10

    1.2.1   Transactional Databases   10

    1.2.2   Decision Support Databases   11

    1.2.3   Hybrid Databases   13

1.3   Conclusion   14

Chapter 2   The Pieces of the Relational Data Model   15

2.1   Why Discuss the Pieces?   16

2.2   Tables   17

    2.2.1   Columns or Fields   18

    2.2.2   Rows   30

2.3   Relationships   31
   2.3.1   Representing Relationships in an ERD   31
   2.3.2   Keys to Enforce Referential Integrity   41
2.4   Indexes   51
   2.4.1   What is an Index?   51
   2.4.2   Alternate Indexing   52
   2.4.3   Types of Indexes   53
   2.4.4   Different Ways to Build Indexes   56
2.5   Specialized Objects   57
2.6   Conclusion   60

Chapter 3   Intuitive Relational Data Modeling and Normalization   61
3.1   Normalization and Normal Forms   63
   3.1.1   Defining the Normal Forms   63
3.2   Intuitive Database Modeling   65
   3.2.1   Defining Data Modeling Intuitively   66
   3.2.2   Master-Detail Relationship   67
   3.2.3   Dynamic-Static Relationship   73
   3.2.4   Advanced Relationships   79
3.3   Data Model Design with Normalization   87
   3.3.1   Anomalies   88
   3.3.2   Dependency and Determinants   89
   3.3.3   Defining Normal Forms Again   93
   3.3.4   1st Normal Form   94
   3.3.5   2nd Normal Form   96
   3.3.6   3rd Normal Form   98
   3.3.7   Advanced Normalization Beyond 3rd Normal Form   100
3.4   Conclusion   113

Chapter 4   Reading and Writing Relational Data with SQL   115
4.1   What is SQL?   116
   4.1.1   The Origins of SQL   117
   4.1.2   SQL for Different Databases   118
   4.1.3   Introducing SQL   118
4.2   Querying a Database Using SELECT   120
   4.2.1   Filtering with the WHERE Clause   122
   4.2.2   Sorting with the ORDER BY Clause   126

4.2.3	Aggregating with the GROUP BY Clause	127
4.2.4	Join Queries	128
4.2.5	Nested Queries	136
4.2.6	Composite Queries	137
4.3	Changing Data in a Database	138
4.3.1	Understanding Transactions	139
4.4	Changing Database Metadata	141
4.5	Conclusion	146

Chapter 5   Advanced Relational Database Modeling   **147**

5.1	Understanding Denormalization	149
5.1.1	Normal Form Definitions	149
5.1.2	Intuitive Data Modeling Definitions	150
5.1.3	Denormalizing Granularity Created in Chapter 3	151
5.1.4	Denormalization Using Specialized Database Objects	156
5.1.5	Denormalization Tricks	158
5.2	Understanding the Object Database Model	160
5.3	Introducing the Data Warehouse Model	165
5.4	Conclusion	167

Chapter 6   Understanding Data Warehouse Database Modeling   **169**

6.1	What Is a Data Warehouse?	170
6.1.1	The Relational Database Model and Data Warehouses	172
6.2	The Dimensional Database Model	174
6.2.1	What Is a Star Schema?	175
6.2.2	What Is a Snowflake Schema?	176
6.2.3	Kimball and Inmon on Data Warehousing	181
6.3	Data Warehouse Modeling	183
6.3.1	Understanding Business Processes	184
6.3.2	Granularity	184
6.3.3	Commonly Occurring Types of Dimension Tables	186
6.3.4	Understanding the Basics of Fact Tables	189
6.4	Conclusion	195

Chapter 7   Modeling for BigData Databases   **197**

7.1	Dimensional Modeling and Staging Databases in the Age of BigData	198
7.1.1	The Data Vault Model	199

7.1.2 The Anchor Model 203

7.1.3 Connecting the Dots from Relations and
Dimensions Through to BigData 204

7.2 What Is BigData Modeling? 206

7.2.1 Some Useful BigData Modeling Terminology 206

7.2.2 Comparing ACID and BASE Consistency Models 209

7.2.3 Risks with BigData Modeling 211

7.2.4 Schema on Read (Schema-Less) 212

7.3 Four Main Types of BigData Modeling Architectures 216

7.3.1 Columnar BigData Modeling 216

7.3.2 Key-Value Store Data Modeling 221

7.3.3 Document Collection Data Modeling 231

7.3.4 Graph Data Modeling 238

7.4 Conclusion 242

Index **243**

List of Figures

Figure 1.1   The evolution of relational database modeling techniques.   2

Figure 1.2   The hierarchical database model.   4

Figure 1.3   The network database model.   5

Figure 1.4   The relational database model.   6

Figure 1.5   The relational database model—a picture of the data
from Figure 1.4.   7

Figure 1.6   The object database model.   8

Figure 2.1   Table columns express the metadata dimension.   17

Figure 2.2   Table rows duplicate the set of columns into the tuples
or data dimension.   18

Figure 2.3   Raw data has structure applied to it to create
structured data.   19

Figure 2.4   The vertical structure of the EDITION table showing
columns, constraints and datatypes.   20

Figure 2.5   Fixed-length strings and variable-length strings.   22

Figure 2.6   Integer, decimal, and floating-point numeric datatypes.   25

Figure 2.7   Adding values to floating point datatype columns.   26

Figure 2.8   Dates with timestamps and dates without timestamps.   27

Figure 2.9   Rows repeat table column structure.   30

Figure 2.10 An ERD or entity relationship diagram of related tables.   31

Figure 2.11 A crow's foot represents the many side of a one-to-many
relationship in an ERD.   32

Figure 2.12 A one-to-one or zero relationship implies one or zero RANK for each EDITION. 33

Figure 2.13 A one-to-one relationship implies exactly one entry in both tables. 34

Figure 2.14 One-to-many implies one entry to many entries between two tables. 34

Figure 2.15 One-to-many implies one entry to many entries between two tables. 35

Figure 2.16 Resolving a many-to-many relationship with a new table. 36

Figure 2.17 Resolving a many-to-many relationship into a new table. 37

Figure 2.18 One implies a row must be present. zero implies that a row can be present. 38

Figure 2.19 A one-to-one or zero relationship. 39

Figure 2.20 Identifying, non-identifying, and dependent relationships. 40

Figure 2.21 A primary key uniquely identifies a row in a table. 42

Figure 2.22 A foreign key is used to link back to the primary key of a parent table. 45

Figure 2.23 Band names, tracks, and silly descriptions. 49

Figure 2.24 Band names, tracks and silly descriptions represented in various ERDs. 50

Figure 2.25 A BTree index. 54

Figure 2.26 A Bitmap Index. 55

Figure 3.1 A table that is not normalized or modeled at all. 68

Figure 3.2 The AUTHORSBOOKS table with no break-down or normalization applied. 69

Figure 3.3 Using comma-delimited lists to represent a repeating group. 70

Figure 3.4 A master-detail relationship creates two tables for AUTHORSBOOKS. 70

Figure 3.5 Primary keys and the foreign key pointers between master and detail tables. 71

Figure 3.6 Authors and their books described by a master-detail relationship. 72

Figure 3.7 The BOOK table contains repeating values that can be separated out. 74

Figure 3.8   Separate information using the differences between
dynamic and static data.   75

Figure 3.9   Create many-to-one relationships between dynamic and
static tables.   75

Figure 3.10 Primary keys in static tables are copied to the BOOK
dynamic table as part of the dynamic table composite
primary key.   76

Figure 3.11 Non-identifying relationships prevent foreign primary
keys from identifying objects uniquely.   77

Figure 3.12 Books plus their respective publishers and subjects
are better organized with dynamic-static many-to-one
relationships.   78

Figure 3.13 Resolving a many-to-many relationship into a new table.   80

Figure 3.14 A many-to-many relationship finds duplicate rows when
unique rows are sought.   80

Figure 3.15 Spreading out the values in a many-to-many relationship. 81

Figure 3.16 Amalgamating duplication from more than one table.   82

Figure 3.17 A transitive dependency separation from one table to
a new table.   84

Figure 3.18 Remove transitively dependent calculated columns.   85

Figure 3.19 Removing NULL columns to new tables.   86

Figure 3.20 Removing NULL valued columns into a new table.   86

Figure 3.21 Splitting multiple NULLs in multiple new tables is
too much granularization.   87

Figure 3.22 Functional dependency and the determinant.   89

Figure 3.23 A table with five and possibly more candidate keys.   90

Figure 3.24 Full functional dependence.   91

Figure 3.25 Multiple valued dependencies   92

Figure 3.26 A table with no normalization.   94

Figure 3.27 1st normal form transformation of the SALES table in
Figure 3.26.   95

Figure 3.28 Two tables in 1st normal form.   97

Figure 3.29 Four tables in 2nd normal form.   98

Figure 3.30 Four tables in 2nd normal form.   99

Figure 3.31 Five tables in 3rd normal form.   100

Figure 3.32 Using Boyce-Codd normal form to separate all candidate keys into separate tables. 102

Figure 3.33 Multi-valued lists not in 4th normal form. 104

Figure 3.34 Multiple multi-valued dependencies equates to multiple many-to-many. 104

Figure 3.35 Multiple unrelated multi-valued dependencies can produce a lot of duplication 105

Figure 3.36 Data for the classic example 4th normal form as shown in Figure 3.35. 106

Figure 3.37 A pre-5th normal form three-column composite primary key table. 108

Figure 3.38 A 5th normal form transformation. 108

Figure 3.39 5th normal form transformations sometimes remove duplicates and prevent update anomalies. 109

Figure 3.40 5th normal form transformations must return rows identical to the pre-5th normal form transformation when joined. 111

Figure 4.1 The online book store relational database model. 144

Figure 5.1 Remove NULL column tables. 152

Figure 5.2 Denormalizing BCNF (remove separate candidate key tables). 153

Figure 5.3 Denormalization of 5th normal form cyclic dependencies. 154

Figure 5.4 Removal of amalgamated columns in an extra table. 155

Figure 5.5 Denormalization of a transitive dependence resolution table. 155

Figure 5.6 Removal of calculated columns. 156

Figure 5.7 Remove dynamic-static relationships back into a single static table. 157

Figure 5.8 Denormalize by copying columns to reduce join sizes. 159

Figure 5.9 Denormalization using summary columns in parent tables. 160

Figure 5.10 Comparing a relational database model with an equivalent object model as shown in Figure 5.11. 162

Figure 5.11 Comparing an object database model with a relational model as shown in Figure 5.10. 163

Figure 5.12 The SUBJECT table contains a parent-child hierarchy. 164

Figure 5.13 A data warehouse model star schema. 167

Figure 6.1   The OLTP relational database model for books.   174
Figure 6.2   The REVIEW table fact-dimensional structure.   175
Figure 6.3   The REVIEW fact-dimensional structure is a star schema. 176
Figure 6.4   The SALE table fact-dimensional structure.   177
Figure 6.5   The SALE fact-dimensional structure as a
              snowflake schema.   178
Figure 6.6   A denormalized SALE table fact-dimensional structure.   178
Figure 6.7   The SALE fact-dimensional structure denormalized into
              a star schema.   179
Figure 6.8   Modern data warehouse 3rd normal form architecture.   182
Figure 6.9   A time dimension entity.   186
Figure 6.10   Adding the time dimension to the facts.   188
Figure 6.11   Location dimensions are commonly used to analyze
              data by region.   189
Figure 6.12   Adding a location dimension to facts.   190
Figure 6.13   An OLTP relational database model.   192
Figure 6.14   A data warehouse snowflake schema.   193
Figure 6.15   A data warehouse snowflake schema ERD.   193
Figure 6.16   A data warehouse star schema.   194
Figure 6.17   A data warehouse star schema ERD.   194
Figure 7.1   Modern data warehouse 3rd normal form staging plus
              warehouse architecture, repeated from Figure 6.8.   198
Figure 7.2   A simple star schema for books and customers,
              repeated from Figure 6.6.   200
Figure 7.3   A data vault form of the star schema as shown in
              Figure 7.2.   201
Figure 7.4   A flattened BigData schema showing separate
              equivalents of separate business functions.   207
Figure 7.5   A simple sample BigData model ecosystem.   208
Figure 7.6   NoSQL database vendors in recent years, with some
              MPP data warehouses added.   213
Figure 7.7   The pre-relational hierarchical database model.   214
Figure 7.8   The pre-relational network database model.   215
Figure 7.9   Denormalizing multiple functional datamarts into a
              single BigData table.   217
Figure 7.10   A visual representation of rows stored in a table.   218

Figure 7.11 An index is a subset of columns of the entire column
set from a table.   219

Figure 7.12 Converting a relational table to a key-value store table.   223

Figure 7.13 A simple fact table star schema structure.   224

Figure 7.14 Visualizing a document-collection database looks like
a hierarchy.   234

Figure 7.15 A simplistic visual representation of a document
collection database model.   235

Figure 7.16 Visualizing a JSON object into a document
collection model.   236

Figure 7.17 A simple social graph model showing relationships
between people.   240

Figure 7.18 A social graph augmented by interests into a social
interest graph.   241

Figure 7.19 Graphs are model data not metadata, but are used as
mathematical abstractions.   241

Preface

The original purpose of this book when it was written 15 years ago was to attempt to simplify relational database modeling a little, by presenting the standard approach to normalization and then adding a more simplistic intuitive approach to building relational database models. The second edition was self-published and added data warehouse modeling. This third edition has now added some very brief coverage of BigData logical modeling—brief because there is not much to logical data modeling in BigData databases as they are often schema-less, which means that BigData databases do not have schemas embedded into the database itself—they have no metadata and thus not much of a logical data model.

This book begins with relational data modeling and ends with BigData data modeling, the latter of which there is not much to. A road map includes relational modeling evolution and brief introductions to data warehousing and BigData modeling. Next is a break-down of the elements of pieces of what makes up a relational data model, followed by a comparison between standard normalization, along with a more simplistic intuitive approach to data modeling that a layman can follow and understand.

Next is a brief chapter on how to use the basic programming language SQL (Structured Query Language), which reads and writes a relational database and which is fundamental to data modeling because it helps in understanding how the model is used; real-world practical application can be educationally effective for many. The last three chapters cover important modern world topics in addition to the relational model, including denormalization that leads into data warehouses, and finally BigData database data modeling.

The following link contains extra chapters and information not included in this printed title, mostly a case study that was eliminated from the third edition because it only covers relational data modeling:

www.oracletroubleshooter.com/datamodeling.html

I can be contacted at gavin@oracletroubleshooter.com

Disclaimer Notice. Please note that the content of this book is made available AS IS. I am in no way responsible or liable for any mishaps as a result of using this information, in any form or environment.

About the Author

Gavin Powell is a veteran IT practitioner and author of a number of Oracle publications. Gavin has extensive experience in many databases, including over a decade working with Oracle databases.

Gavin has authored the following books:

- *Oracle Performance Tuning for $10^9 R2$*
- *Oracle SQL Jumpstart with Examples (with Carol McCullough-Dieter)*
- *Oracle Data Warehouse Tuning for 10gR2*
- *Oracle High-Performance Tuning for 9i and 10g*
- *Working with GoldenGate 12c*

Chapter 1

The Evolution of Relational Database Modeling

A page of history is worth a volume of logic.[*]

—Oliver Wendell Holmes

*Why a theory was devised and how it is now applied
can be more significant than the theory itself.*

The relational database model evolved into what it is today to keep pace with commercial demands over the past 50 years. The various data models that came before the relational database model, such as the hierarchical and network database models, were only partial solutions to a never-ending problem—how to store and retrieve data and how to do it accurately and efficiently. The relational database model does have strengths and weaknesses but is currently the most flexible solution for both storage and retrieval of large quantities of transactional information.

In the world of data modeling, it is essential to understand how the different data models evolved into the relational database model we have today, because understanding the relational database model from its roots helps in understanding the critical problems that the relational database model helps to solve.

---

[*] https://quotes.yourdictionary.com/author/oliver-wendell-holmes-jr/164969

This chapter covers:

- The evolution of database modeling
- Hierarchical and network database modeling
- From relational to object and object-relational database modeling
- Some general approaches to database modeling
- Brief introductory notes on data warehouses and BigData

1.1 From File Systems to Object-Relational Databases

The evolution of database modeling occurred as a result of a need to solve various problems, whose most obvious first solution was to use file systems to store files as flat files on disk, which were simple text or binary files. The first model structure to evolve was called the *hierarchical database model*, which was used to enforce structure onto different subsets of data, in which each subset group was contained within a parent. The next thing that appeared on the database scene was the *network database model*, improving on the hierarchical database model by providing solutions to some of the issues that the hierarchical model could not address. The ultimate in relational database modeling evolution was the *object-relational database model* as an extension of the *object database model*.

Figure 1.1 shows a picture of the evolutionary process of relational data modeling over time, from around the late 1940s through to and beyond

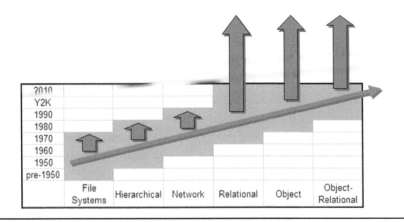

Figure 1.1   The evolution of relational database modeling techniques.

the turn of the millennium, more than 50 years later. Some software has longevity, in that there might even be some network and hierarchical databases that are still in use, and perhaps even the odd file system structured database implementation.

1.1.1 File Systems

Using a file system database model implies very few modeling techniques other some data typing analysis, and the database is stored in flat files in a file system utilizing the structure of the operating system alone. Data can be stored in individual files or multiple files. Any relationships and validation between different flat files would have to be programmed in manually and limited only by the power and sophistication of that manual programming.

1.1.2 The Hierarchical Database Model

The hierarchical database model is an inverted, tree-like structure, in which each child table has a single parent table and each parent table can have multiple child tables.

> A table is the most basic container in a relational database, containing both the definition of data and the data itself.

A child table can only exist if its parent table exists, and thus child tables are completely dependent on their respective parent tables—any entries in child tables can only exist where corresponding parent entries exist in parent tables. The result of this structure is that the hierarchical database model can support one-to-many relationships, such as a project having many employees working on a single project at once; but the hierarchical model cannot support many-to-many relationships, such as many employees working on multiple projects at the same time, where the unique employee project combinations cannot be found.

Figure 1.2 shows an example hierarchical database model in which every task is part of a project, which belongs to a manager, which is part of a division, which is part of a company. The disadvantages of the hierarchical database model are that any access must originate at the root node. In the hierarchical database in Figure 1.2, you always have to begin a search with

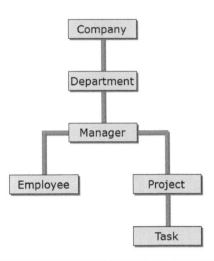

Figure 1.2   The hierarchical database model.

a company and eventually have to search the entire database in order to locate and retrieve a single task—that is a lot of searching. As can be seen, direct many-to-many relationships are not supported, so a task cannot be assigned to an employee directly, but only through the parent objects of project and manager—the back and forth processing can be complicated and time consuming, and as a result, much of this processing must be hard coded within applications, obscuring data relationships and making maintenance more difficult.

1.1.3 The Network Database Model

The network database model is essentially a refinement of the hierarchical database model, allowing child tables to have more than one parent, creating a networked like table structure. The effect of multiple parent tables for each child allows for many-to-many relationships, but those relationships are hard coded and they limit flexibility.

Figure 1.3 shows managers having multiple parents, and in this case those parents are company and department. In other words, the network model in Figure 1.3 is taking into account the fact that not only does each department within a company have a manager, but also that each company has an overall manager or CEO. Figure 1.3 also shows the addition of type or static data tables, in which employees can be defined as being of different types, such as full-time, part-time, or even contract employ-ees. Most importantly to note from Figure 1.3 is the new Assignment table allowing for the assignment of tasks to employees. The creation of the assignment table is a direct result of the addition of multiple parent capability in the evolution from the hierarchical to the network model. The relationship between the employee and task tables is a many-to-many rela-tionship, because each employee can be assigned multiple tasks, and each task can be assigned to multiple employees. The assignment table resolves a problem by allowing a unique definition for the combination of employee and task as the assignment of a task to a particular employee.

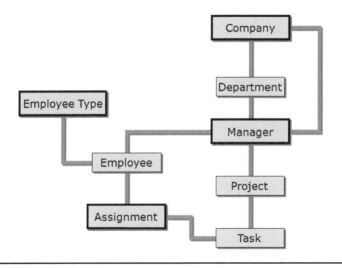

Figure 1.3   The network database model.

1.1.4 The Relational Database Model

The relational database model improves on the hierarchical and network database models by lending a two-dimensional structure to data. The rela-tional database model does not completely abandon the hierarchy of data, as can be seen in Figure 1.4, because in the relational model any table can be accessed directly without having to access a parent object, as would have to be done with the hierarchical model. The trick is to know what to look for, such as employees or managers; if you want to find the address of a specific employee, you have to know which employee to look for, such as

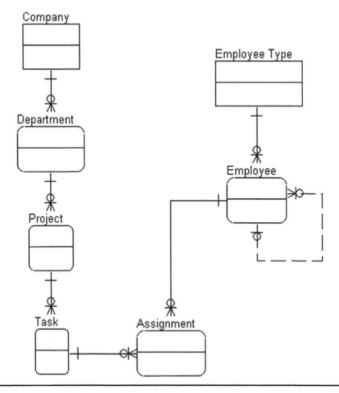

Figure 1.4 The relational database model.

a person's name, but you can also examine all employees first in order to find a specific person.

Another benefit of the relational database model is that any tables can be linked together, regardless of their position in the hierarchy. There should be a sensible link between two tables, but one is not restricted by a strict hierarchical structure, and thus a table can be limited to both any number of parent tables and any number of child tables.

Figure 1.5 shows a small example section of the relational database model shown in Figure 1.4, describing some data that could be contained within the project and the task tables. The PROJECT_ID column in the project table uniquely identifies each project in the project table. The relationship between the project and task tables is a one-to-many relationship linking with the PROJECT_ID column (the PROJECT_ID column is present in both the project and task tables, as shown in Figure 1.5), duplicated from the project table to the task table. As can be seen in Figure 1.5, the first three entries in the Task table are all part of the *Software sales data mart* project, showing three tasks contained within a single project, which is a one-to-many relationship between project and tasks (one project has many possible tasks).

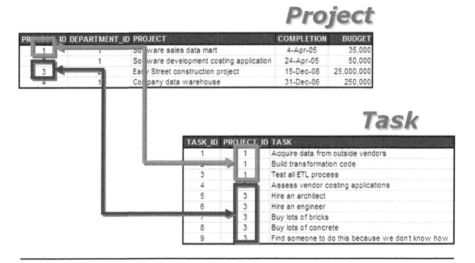

Figure 1.5   The relational database model—a picture of the data from Figure 1.4.

1.1.5 The Object Database Model

An object database model gives a three-dimensional structure to data, wherein any item in a database can be retrieved from any point, and very rapidly—as long as it is small in size. In other words, the relational database model lends itself to retrieval of groups of rows in sets, and in two dimensions. In contrast, the object database model is very efficient for finding small but unique items, consequently, the object database model performs very poorly when retrieving more than a single item, such as when doing reporting, because it has to search for many individual items repeatedly; but it is extremely fast when updating a single object, such as an employee's name.

In the competition between the relational and object models, the relational database model is reasonably good at working with small chunks of data as well as larger chunks in something like a report, and so the relational model tends to win out over the object model in the end for most commercial applications.

The object database model does resolve some of the more obscure complexities of the relational database model, such as the removal of the need for types (static data) as well as many-to-many relationship resolution tables; types and many-to-many relationships are built in to an object structure. Figure 1.6 shows an example object database model structure equivalent of the relational database model structure shown in Figure 1.4. The assignment of tasks to employees is catered to by using a collection inclusion in the manager, employee, and contractor employee specialization classes, which removes the need for many-to-many relationships. Also note that the different types of employees are catered to by using specializations of the employee class, which in this case are types of employees that include full-time employees, part-time employees, and contractors.

The other benefit of the object database model is its inherent ability to manage and allow for the break down in complexity of extremely complex

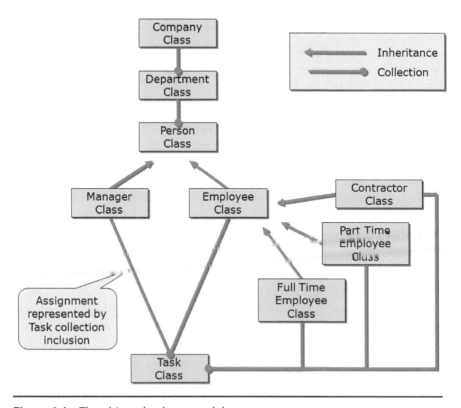

Figure 1.6   The object database model.

applications and database models, in which highly complex elements can and should be broken down into their most basic parts; the result is often called *black-box objects* that are self contained and can be made to function properly without having any dependencies on any other objects. In other words, if you can figure out how all the little pieces work individually, then it can often make the big picture much clearer and easier to understand. Why? Because once you understand and resolve the small parts, you do not have to think about what is in those smaller parts, and you can reuse them at will later on and only remain concerned about how the parts fit together into a working object model. So object modeling often becomes a matter of how a problem is approached, building pieces and putting them together, and not having to be concerned about the contents of each individual piece of a puzzle, as you solve problems one by one and on a successively larger scale.

The object database model discussion is included because many modern applications are written using object methodology–based SDKs (Software Development Kits), such as Java® and Microsoft®'s .Net products. One of the biggest sticking points for performance between object-based applications and relational databases is the performance of the mapping process between the two structural types: object-designed applications and relational databases underpinning them. Object structures and relational structures are completely different, and it is therefore useful to have some understanding of object database modeling techniques in order to allow development of efficient use of relational databases by object-built applications. In addition, there are some evolutionary steps within relational database modeling techniques that are very useful to object applications, so it is useful for you to understand something about objects and object data modeling.

1.1.6 The Object-Relational Database Model

One could imagine an object database model to be somewhat spherical or three dimensional in nature, because it allows access to unique elements anywhere within a database structure, and with extremely high performance for very small amounts of data—especially if you know exactly what to look for. On the contrary, the object database model performs extremely poorly when retrieving more than a single data item, and so object databases are not very good at creating reports across large sets of data—and this is because data is not organized sequentially in an object database. The object-relational database model was devised by relational database vendors in answer to potential competition to their relational databases from competing object database vendors; however, object-relational databases do not perform well when including objects. In an object-relational database model, object database modeling capabilities are included into relational databases, not the other way around, with many relational databases now allowing object features such as storage of binary objects such as images and audio files, as well as some limited object coding capabilities.

1.2 General Types of Database Models

Database models fall into three general categories: (1) transactional (OLTP), (2) decision support systems (DSS), or (3) a hybrid of the two.

1.2.1 Transactional Databases

A transactional database is one that has lots of small changes made to it by small transactions, which makes for a transaction-driven database. So the primary function of a transactional database is adding new data, changing plus deleting existing data, and reading data—all in small amounts by lots of different people all at the same time; those small chunks are usually individual records, such as read a single customer, add a new customer, change an existing customer name, or deleting a person who is no longer a customer. Traditionally, there are two types of transactional databases:

- **Client-Server Database.** A client-server environment was common in the pre-Internet days in which a transactional database serviced users within a single company across a Local Area Network (LAN) or a Wide Area Network (WAN). The number of users could range from as little as one to thousands, depending on the size of the company. The critical factor was a mixture of both individual row change activity and modestly sized reports. Client-server database models typically catered to low concurrency (a known number of users) and low throughput (not much change to the database); the number of users in a single company is more manageable than an online database.

- **OLTP Database**. OLTP means Online Transaction Processing, which means a database that services a potentially massive and unknown number of users on the Internet; all those users can cause problems with concurrency where resources must have a very high level of accessibility and share-ability. The number of users that can be reached over the Internet is an unimaginable order of magnitude larger than that of an in-house company client-server database; so concurrency requirements for OLTP database models explodes well beyond the scope of previous experience with client-server databases.

  For example, a client-server database inside a company services 1,000 users. A company of 1,000 people is small enough to possibly all be located in a single country, and maybe even in the same building in a single city. Therefore, our client-server database services 1,000 people eight hours per day, five days a week, perhaps 50 weeks a year, which is a total of about 2,000 hours per year, per person at any given point during the day. Also consider how many users will be accessing the database at exactly the same millisecond. The answer is probably only 1.

  An OLTP database, on the other hand, can have millions of potential users, 24 hours per day and 365 days per year—think about the size of eBay® or Amazon®—both are a combination of OLTP and data warehouse environments and use many database vendor products and architectures. An OLTP database must be permanently online and concurrently available to many thousands of users every millisecond. If half a million people are watching the home shopping network on television and a website appears offers something for free that everyone wants—how many people hit the home shopping network website at the same time? The quantities of users that an OLTP database have to cater to is potentially staggering, with enormously high levels of concurrent database access.

1.2.2 Decision Support Databases

DSS, or Decision Support Systems, are commonly known as DSS databases, and they do just that—they support decisions, and also decisions at the level of planning and forecasting. There are a few variations of DSS databases:

A cloud-based database or Database and Software as a Service is not really a database type, but rather a delivery method, in that cloud-based databases can be OLTP, even client-server; even data warehouses and BigData databases are now available in the cloud in numerous different forms and from a multitude of different vendors.

- **Data Warehouse Database.** A data warehouse database can use the same data modeling approach as a transactional database model, but it can alternatively use a data model that contains a more end user–friendly structure of facts and dimensions about the business of a company. The facts contain the history of transactions such as the invoices and notes in a simple accounting system; the dimensions describe static details about the facts, such as the names and addresses of customers and suppliers. Data warehouses often contain many years of historical data in order to provide effective forecasting capabilities by allowing for searching over archival type data to help make future business decisions based on past trends and patterns. The result is that data warehouses can become excessively large, even millions of times larger than the corresponding OLTP source databases. The OLTP database is known as the *source database*, because the OLTP database is the database in which all the transactional information for the data warehouse originates; the data warehouse is the *target database*. As data becomes not current in an OLTP database, it is moved to a data warehouse database and deleted from the OLTP database.
- **Data Mart.** A data mart is a small subset of a larger data warehouse and is usually a single functional transaction record (a fact table) among many fact tables in a larger data warehouse, such as the sales or buying history of a company. A data mart uses the same fact dimensional database modeling technique as a data warehouse does, and data marts are created to break up data warehouses into separately or semi-separately usable business functions when a data warehouse becomes too large to manage.
- **Reporting Database.** A reporting database is a data warehouse type of database but containing only active and not historical or archived data, and reports are simple records of current activity for the business of an organization. As a result, reporting databases are usually much smaller than data warehouses but can still use a data

warehouse fact-dimensional structure, because a data warehouse database model builds data into the order and sets that help reports to run much faster than they would in an OLTP database—and it also removes processing and resource conflict from an OLTP database.

- **BigData, Analytics, and Business Intelligence.** BigData data stores and ecosystems are generally very large databases that separate themselves from data warehouses by completely discarding schemas and internal database logical structure in favor of performance, largely because of the huge amounts of raw data involved. BigData data modeling will be covered in Chapter 7.

Data warehouse databases are typically less flexible with respect to maintenance because they can get so incredibly large, and maintenance on large amounts of disk storage space takes time. OLTP databases are more flexible but can be cripplingly slow when doing tasks such as reporting, and they are impossible for any kind of trend analysis work. Data warehouse modeling will be covered in detail in later chapters.

1.2.3 Hybrid Databases

A hybrid database is a mixture containing both OLTP-type concurrency requirements, in addition to large-scale full table scanning needs, such as for reporting databases, data warehouses, and even BigData ecosystems. In less demanding environments or companies running smaller operations, a smaller hybrid database is often a more cost-effective option simply because there is one rather than two databases—fewer machines, fewer software licenses, fewer people, the list goes on.

OLTP databases require very efficient memory and CPUs with very specific random disk seek access. On the contrary, other database types such as data warehouses require lots of very fast and defragmented disk space access with a single seek and a very large read for each access operation (full table scans). In short, the two do not really mix very well because their requirements cause them to compete with each other.

BigData databases store data in multiple ways but with very specific functions, including columnar databases, key-store value stores, hierarchical-type document collections, and network-like graphs; see Chapter 7 for more detail on BigData databases. The point to note is that modern BigData databases have been partially devised in order to attempt to resolve the problems of hybridizing databases—by specializing and removing functionality (schemas) from BigData databases.

1.3 Conclusion

This chapter covered:

- The evolution of database modeling, why and how
- The hierarchical database model
- The network database model
- The relational database model
- The object database model
- The object-relational database model
- Some general types of database modeling
- Brief introductory notes on data warehouses and BigData

The next chapter will explain and examine the pieces of the relational database model.

Chapter 2

The Pieces of the Relational Data Model

Well begun is half done.[*]

—Aristotle

Begin at the beginning by starting with the simple pieces.

This chapter introduces the basics of relational database modeling by discussing and explaining all the various parts and pieces making up a relational database model, as well as all the terminology and phrasing, before you go into reading about building a database.

So far, this book has covered the historical evolution of database models, how different applications and end-user needs affect database type, and what could be called the "art" of database design. Before describing how a data model is built, you need to know what all the pieces are that make up a data model. Tables are the most important piece in the puzzle of the relational database model, for which columns in tables are of less significance but still essential to the semantics of the database model as a whole. You as the reader need a basic knowledge of all the parts and pieces constituting the relational database model, and this chapter describes all those parts and pieces that you need, which will lead you

---

[*] https://www.yourdictionary.com/well-begun-is-half-done#wiktionary

into subsequent chapters covering the process of creating and refining relational database models. All of the constituents of the relational database model help to create an organized logical structure for managing data in a database; that organized logical structure is called *the relational database model.*

This chapter covers:

- Tables
- Columns and rows
- Datatypes
- Validation using constraints
- Relationships
- Keys and constraints
- Indexes
- Specialized objects

Why analyze and discuss the pieces of the relational database model?

2.1 Why Discuss the Pieces?

The objective of this book is to gradually teach an understanding of the relational database model. Chapter 1 covered introductory topics such as database modeling history in order to describe the benefits and reasons for evolution of the relational database model as it exists today. Various aspects of this book have already gone into some detail to describe some very basic and fundamental concepts, but so far the deeply technical details have been avoided. This chapter begins with the detailed parts of the database model; the parts and pieces of a data model include tables, columns, and datatypes, among other objects.

If you already know what a table, a column, a record, and an index are, then you can probably skip reading this chapter if you are really strapped for time. However, do read this chapter if you have the time, because there are concepts, ideas, and object aspects of data modeling described here that you will not find in most books of this nature. I have taken the liberty of expanding on the basic structure of the relational database model and added little bits and pieces here and there, such as materialized views and auto counter sequences. For example, even though materialized views are not a part of the normalization process used to create a relational database model, they can have a most profound effect on the behavior of data warehouses but are sometimes used in OLTP databases as well.

> Normalization is a step-by-step methodology used to divide data into separate tables, according to a set of mathematically based rules. So at this stage in this book, assume that the term *normalization* implies that new tables are being created or being transformed (normalized) into more refined versions of existing tables.

So let's begin with the most obvious and fundamental of relational database objects: the table.

2.2 Tables

In data modeling theory, a table is a bucket into which data is organized. The idea of the relational database model and normalization is that data in a specific table is directly related to all other items in that same table in one dimension. So Figure 2.1 shows horizontally how each column's data values are related to other column values on each row—where each book has an ISBN, an author, a publisher, a title; is in a specific book genre; and was printed on a specific date.

ISBN	AUTHOR	PUBLISHER	TITLE	GENRE	PRINTED
459947 0081	James Blish	Overlook Press	Cities In Flight	Science Fiction	
345333920	Larry Niven	Ballantine Books	Ringworld	Science Fiction	11-Nov-20
345336275	Isaac Azimov	Ballantine Books	Foundation	Science Fiction	31-Jul-86
345438353	James Blish	Ballantine Books	A Case of Conscience	Science Fiction	
553293362	Isaac Azimov	Bantam Books	Second Foundation	Science Fiction	
553278398	Isaac Azimov	Spectra	Prelude to Foundation	Science Fiction	
553293389	Isaac Azimov	Spectra	Foundation's Edge	Science Fiction	
553293370	Isaac Azimov	Spectra	Foundation and Empire	Science Fiction	
893402095	Isaac Azimov	L P Books	Foundation	Science Fiction	31-May-79
345323440	Larry Niven	Del Rey Books	Footfall	Science Fiction	31-Jul-96
345334787	Isaac Azimov	Del Rey Books	Foundation	Science Fiction	31-Dec-85
345308999	Isaac Azimov	Del Rey Books	Foundation	Science Fiction	28-Feb-83
5553673224	Isaac Azimov	Books on Tape	Foundation	Science Fiction	31-Jan-20
5557076654	Isaac Azimov	Books on Tape	Foundation	Science Fiction	31-Jan-51
246118318	Isaac Azimov	HarperCollins Publishers	Foundation	Science Fiction	28-Apr-83
449208133	Larry Niven	Fawcett Books	Lucifer's Hammer	Science Fiction	31-May-85
425130215	Kurt Vonnegut	Berkley Publishing Group	Hocus Pocus	Modern American	30-Nov-91

Figure 2.1   Table columns express the metadata dimension.

ISBN	AUTHOR	PUBLISHER	TITLE	GENRE	PRINTED
1585670081	James Blish	Overlook ss	Cities in Flight	Science Fiction	
345333926	Larry Niven	Ballantin oks	Ringworld	Science Fiction	30-Nov-90
345336275	Isaac Azimov	Ballantin oks	Foundation	Science Fiction	31-Jul-86
345438353	James Blish	Ballantin oks	A Case of Conscience	Science Fiction	
553293362	Isaac Azimov	Bantam E s	Second Foundation	Science Fiction	
553278398	Isaac Azimov	Spectra	Prelude to Foundation	Science Fiction	
553293389	Isaac Azimov	Spectra	Foundation's Edge	Science Fiction	
553293370	Isaac Azimov	Spectra	Foundation and Empire	Science Fiction	
893402095	Isaac Azimov	L P Book:	Foundation	Science Fiction	31-May-79
345323440	Larry Niven	Del Rey E s	Footfall	Science Fiction	31-Jul-96
345334787	Isaac Azimov	Del Rey E s	Foundation	Science Fiction	31-Dec-85
345308999	Isaac Azimov	Del Rey E s	Foundation	Science Fiction	28-Feb-83
5553673224	Isaac Azimov	Books on e	Foundation	Science Fiction	31-Jan-20
5557076654	Isaac Azimov	Books on e	Foundation	Science Fiction	31-Jan-51
246118318	Isaac Azimov	HarperCo Publishers	Foundation	Science Fiction	28-Apr-83
449208133	Larry Niven	Fawcett E s	Lucifer's Hammer	Science Fiction	31-May-85
425130215	Kurt Vonnegut	Berkley P shing Group	Hocus Pocus	Modern American	30-Nov-91

Figure 2.2   Table rows duplicate the set of columns into the tuples or data dimension.

Rows are repeated over and over again in another dimension (vertically), which duplicate column structures into the vertical dimension, as exaggerated by the enlargement as shown in Figure 2.2.

A table is effectively a structure containing columns across it in one dimension (horizontally), which defines the structure of rows repeatedly added to that table. In other words, all rows in the same tables have the same column structure applied to them. Figure 2.3 shows a picture demonstrating a pile of books on the left, passed through a table structure represented by the miniature ERD in the center of Figure 2.3, which models the data shown on the bottom right of Figure 2.3.

So tables contain columns and rows. Columns apply structure to rows (horizontally), whereas rows duplicate column structure an indefinite number of times as rows (vertically).

2.2.1 Columns or Fields

A column and a field are two different terms for the same thing in database modeling. A column applies structure and definition to a chunk of data within each repeated row. Data is not necessarily repeated on every row, but the structure of columns is applied to each row. So data on each row can be different, both for the row as a whole, and for each column value.

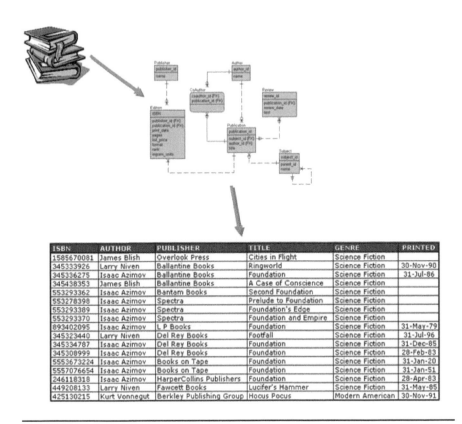

ISBN	AUTHOR	PUBLISHER	TITLE	GENRE	PRINTED
1585670081	James Blish	Overlook Press	Cities in Flight	Science Fiction	
345333926	Larry Niven	Ballantine Books	Ringworld	Science Fiction	30-Nov-90
345336275	Isaac Azimov	Ballantine Books	Foundation	Science Fiction	31-Jul-86
345438353	James Blish	Ballantine Books	A Case of Conscience	Science Fiction	
553293362	Isaac Azimov	Bantam Books	Second Foundation	Science Fiction	
553278398	Isaac Azimov	Spectra	Prelude to Foundation	Science Fiction	
553293389	Isaac Azimov	Spectra	Foundation's Edge	Science Fiction	
553293370	Isaac Azimov	Spectra	Foundation and Empire	Science Fiction	
893402095	Isaac Azimov	L P Books	Foundation	Science Fiction	31-May-79
345323440	Larry Niven	Del Rey Books	Footfall	Science Fiction	31-Jul-96
345334787	Isaac Azimov	Del Rey Books	Foundation	Science Fiction	31-Dec-85
345308999	Isaac Azimov	Del Rey Books	Foundation	Science Fiction	28-Feb-83
5553673224	Isaac Azimov	Books on Tape	Foundation	Science Fiction	31-Jan-20
5557076654	Isaac Azimov	Books on Tape	Foundation	Science Fiction	31-Jan-51
246118318	Isaac Azimov	HarperCollins Publishers	Foundation	Science Fiction	28-Apr-83
449208133	Larry Niven	Fawcett Books	Lucifer's Hammer	Science Fiction	31-May-85
425130215	Kurt Vonnegut	Berkley Publishing Group	Hocus Pocus	Modern American	30-Nov-91

Figure 2.3   Raw data has structure applied to it to create structured data.

Note the use of the term *can be* rather than *is*, implying that there can be duplication across both columns and rows, depending on requirements and constraints and if the table is normalized.

> A constraint is a special restriction in a relational database in which a rule is placed on a column value, such as not allowing a column's value to be set to NULL.

When a value is constrained, it is restricted to having certain values. Figure 2.4 shows a description of the columns in the EDITION table, in which the second box showing NOT NULL for the first three columns specifies that the ISBN, PUBLISHER_ID, and PUBLICATION_ID columns can never contain NULL values in any row.

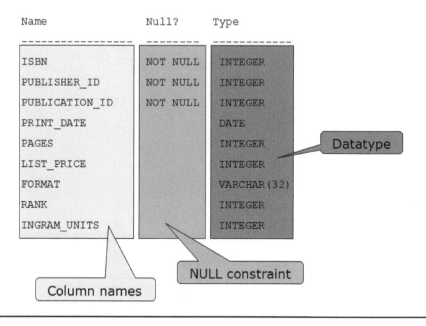

Figure 2.4   The vertical structure of the EDITION table showing columns, constraints and datatypes.

Examine the EDITION table again in Figure 2.4 and note that the left column shows the name of columns in the table where this particular table is used to contain separate editions of the same book. Separate editions of a single book can each be published by different publishers, and so the PUBLISHER_ID column is included in the EDITION table. Another interesting column is the PUBLICATION_ID column, which uniquely identifies a unique book name as stored in the PUBLICATION table. The PUBLICATION table represents each book uniquely, regardless of the existence of multiple editions of the same title, and thus the ISBN uniquely identifies each edition of a book by its unique ISBN. An International Standard Book Number (ISBN) uniquely identifies an edition of a book on an international basis and is the number above the bar code, which is usually printed on the back cover of a printed book.

Datatypes are shown as INTEGER, DATE, or VARCHAR(32) in Figure 2.4, where these three datatypes restrict values to be of certain content and format. The INTEGER datatype only allows whole numbers, which consist of only the digit characters between 0 and 9, with no decimal point character; integers can also be negative. DATE only allows date entries for which specific formatting may apply; most databases will have a default format for date values. If the default format is set to dd/mm/yyyy, then an attempt to set a date value to 12/31/2004 will cause an error, as the day and month values are reversed. Datatypes constrain values in columns in a similar way that a NOT NULL constraint does, based on content of characters and format, making datatypes a form of column value constraining functionality, and so datatypes are also a form of business rule that are applied within a data model.

So columns apply structure to rows, and datatypes apply structure and restrictions to columns and the values stored within those columns. The next step is to go into more detail with datatypes.

2.2.1.1 Datatypes

There are many different types of datatypes, and they can vary often more in name than actual function when examining different datatypes for different database vendors. This section will attempt to describe as many of the different variations of datatypes as possible, but without targeting any specific database vendor.

Datatypes can be divided into three separate sections: (1) simple datatypes, (2) complex datatypes, and (3) specialized datatypes. Simple datatypes are datatypes applying a pattern or value limitation on a single value—a number is a good example. Complex datatypes include any datatypes breaching the object-relational database divide, including things like binary objects and collection arrays. Specifics on complex datatypes are not strictly necessary for this book, because they are more object-oriented than relational in nature, but complex datatypes are becoming more prevalent, so they are included. Specialized datatypes are present in more advanced relational databases catering to inherently structured data such as XML documents, spatial data, multimedia objects, and even dynamically definable datatypes.

Simple Datatypes

Simple datatypes include basic validation and formatting requirements placed onto individual values:

- Strings can be variable-length or fixed-length strings:
  - o **Fixed Length Strings.** A fixed-length strin6g will always store the specified length as declared for the datatype. If the value placed into a fixed-length string is less than the length of the datatype, then the result is padded with space characters (unless it is NULL). For example, the value NY in a CHAR(3) variable would be stored as NY plus a space character. Fixed-length strings are generally only used for short length strings, because a variable-length string requires storage of both value and length, and a short fixed-length string is more efficient to work with than a short variable-length string, because fixed-length strings are more efficient for ensuring fixed record lengths of key values. Figure 2.5 shows an FXCODE column representing a foreign exchange currency code, always returning three characters even when the currency code is less than three characters in length. A case in point is the now Euro

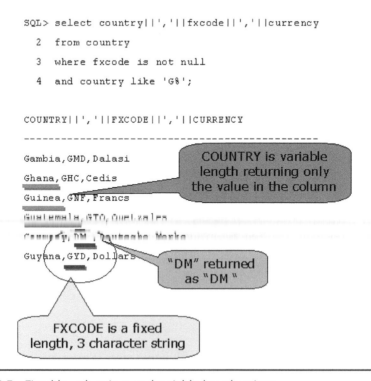

Figure 2.5 Fixed-length strings and variable-length strings.

replaced defunct currency code DM (Deutsche Marks for German currency), returning DM plus a space character yielding a total of three characters.

- o **Variable-Length Strings**. A variable-length string allows storage into a datatype as the actual length of the string, as long as a maximum limit is not exceeded. The length of the string is variable, because when storing a string of length less than the width specified by the datatype, the string is not padded with space characters; only the actual string value is stored. Storing the string XXX into a variable length string datatype of ten characters in length will store the three characters only and not three characters padded by seven spaces, as would be the case for a fixed-length string. Different databases use different naming conventions for variable-length string datatypes, and VARCHAR(n) or TEXT(n) are common naming formats for variable length strings. Figure 2.5 shows variable-length strings for the names of countries (COUNTRY), returning only the names of the countries with no space character padding.

- Numeric datatypes are often the most numerous column datatypes. The following are basic numeric datatype formats:
  - o **Integers**. An integer is a whole number, which has no decimal point and no digits to the right of the decimal point. Some databases allow more detailed specification using small integers and long integers in addition to a standard-sized integer. Figure 2.6 shows three whole number integer datatypes in the columns SINT (small integer), INT (regular length integer), and LONGINT (long integer).
  - o **Fixed-Length Decimals**. A fixed-length decimal is a number, including a decimal point, in which the digits on the right side of the decimal are restricted to a specified number of digits. For example, a DECIMAL(5,2) datatype will allow the values 3.1 and 3.12 but not 3.123, because it allows only 2 digits to the right of the decimal point. However, the value 3.123 might be automatically truncated or rounded to 3.12, depending on the database vendor. Also dependant on the database vendor, the value to the left of the decimal in an example such as number 5 in DECIMAL(5,2) can be interpreted in different ways; in some databases the value 5 limits the number of digits to the left of the decimal point, whereas in other databases 5 limits the total length

of the number, and that total length may include or exclude the decimal point. So in some databases DECIMAL(5,2) would allow 12345.67, but in other databases 12345.67 might not be allowed because the entire number contains more than 5 digits and it might only allow 345.67 or even 45.67 if the decimal is counted as part of the 5 count as a character length limit. In Figure 2.6, assume that DECIMAL(5,2) implies 2 decimals with total digits of 5 at most (excluding the decimal point), and so in Figure 2.6 the columns DECIMALS5_2 and DECIMALS3_0 allow fixed-length decimal values. All INSERT commands adding values to the two DECIMALS5_2 and DECIMALS3_0 columns will fail, because decimal length (overall column length specifications for the datatypes) have not been adhered to.

o **Floating Points**. A floating-point number is just as the name implies: the decimal point floats freely anywhere within the number. In other words, the decimal point can appear anywhere in the number because there is no restriction on how many decimal places are allowed (decimal places is the number of digits to the right of the decimal point). Floating point values can have any number of digits both before and after the decimal point, and they can even have no digits on either side of the decimal point. Values such as 1000, 1000.12345, and 0.8843343223 are all valid floating-point numbers. Floating-point values are likely to be less efficient in storage and retrieval than fixed-length decimals and integers because they are less predictable in terms of record length and otherwise, but floating points are much more flexible. Figure 2.6 shows a 32-byte length floating-point number datatype (column name FLT) and a relatively unlimited length floating-point datatype (column name SFLT).

For most databases, any INSERT commands adding a value into a float column that exceeds the length requirement, such as 32 bytes for SFLT (SFLT is a 5 digit field shown in Figure 2.6), will not produce errors as values are added, but will usually be truncated or converted into exponential (scientific) notation when too large, both as shown in Figure 2.7.

• **Dates and Times**. Dates can be stored as simple dates or dates including timestamp information. In reality, many databases store

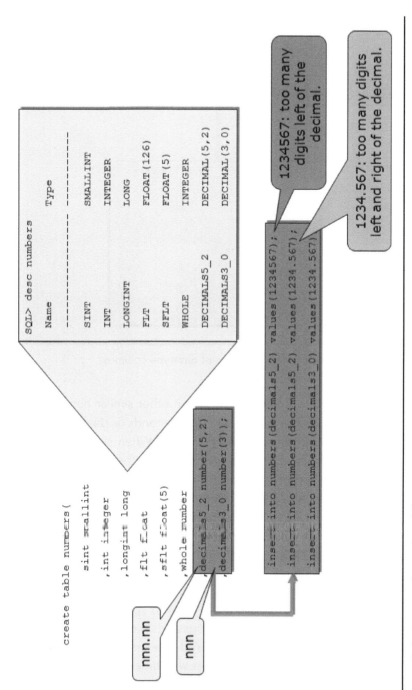

```
create table numbers (
    sint smallint
    ,int integer
    ,longint long
    ,flt float
    ,sflt float(5)
    ,whole number
    ,decimals5_2 number(5,2)
    ,decimals3_0 number(3));
```

nnn.nn

nnn

```
SQL> desc numbers
 Name              Type
 ----------------- -----------------
 SINT              SMALLINT
 INT               INTEGER
 LONGINT           LONG
 FLT               FLOAT(126)
 SFLT              FLOAT(5)
 WHOLE             INTEGER
 DECIMALS5_2       DECIMAL(5,2)
 DECIMALS3_0       DECIMAL(3,0)
```

```
insert into numbers(decimals5_2) values(1234567);
insert into numbers(decimals5_2) values(1234.567);
insert into numbers(decimals3_0) values(1234.567)
```

1234567: too many digits left of the decimal.

1234.567: too many digits left and right of the decimal.

Figure 2.6 Integer, decimal, and floating-point numeric datatypes.

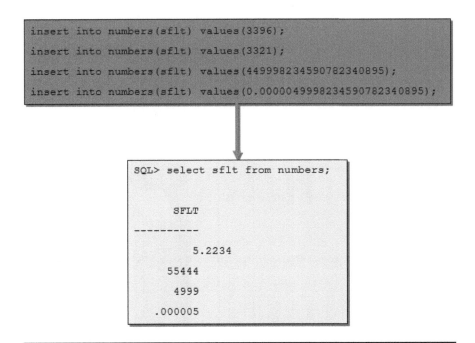

```
insert into numbers(sflt) values(3396);
insert into numbers(sflt) values(3321);
insert into numbers(sflt) values(449998234590782340895);
insert into numbers(sflt) values(0.00000499982345907823408 95);
```

```
SQL> select sflt from numbers;

    SFLT
----------
        5.2234
    55444
    4999
    .000005
```

Figure 2.7   Adding values to floating point datatype columns.

simple dates as a Julian date or some other similar numbering system in which a Julian date is a time in seconds or days from a specified start date, such as January 1, 1960. When simple date values are retrieved from a database and displayed, they are subjected to a default formatting process returning a date formatted as something such as mm/dd/yyyy format (American formatting uses mm/dd/yyyy but other countries use other formats by default); default date formats may or may not include time information as well, depending on the database vendor and default database settings. A date including time information is known as a *timestamp datatype* and displays both date and time information using date formatting configured in a database; timestamps are usually stored specifically as timestamp datatypes, which are stored as strings and do not involve implicit conversions to and from Julian numbered date integer values. Figure 2.8 shows the difference between dates with timestamps and dates without timestamps. Note that Figure 2-8 date formats are dd-mon-yy and dd/mm/yyyy.

```
SQL> select isbn, print_date AS Date,
  2    to_char(print_date,'DD/MM/YYYY HH24:MI:SS') AS TimeStamp
  3  from  edition where print_date is not null;


       ISBN DATE        TIMESTAMP
---------- --------- --------------------
  893402095 31-MAY-79 31/05/1979 00:12:01
  345308999 28-FEB-83 28/02/1983 04:55:03
  345336275 31-JUL-86 31/07/1986 03:44:33
 5557076654 31-JAN-51 31/01/1951 09:41:00
 5553673224 31-JAN-20 31/01/2020 22:15:20
  246118318 28-APR-83 28/04/1983 10:17:10
  345334787 31-DEC-85 31/12/1985 08:13:45
  449208133 31-MAY-85 31/05/1985 00:01:12
  345323440 31-JUL-96 31/07/1996 03:00:30
  345333926 30-NOV-90 30/11/1990 21:04:40
  425130215 30-NOV-91 30/11/1991 16:43:53
```

Database specific format

Timestamp format

Figure 2.8   Dates with timestamps and dates without timestamps.

Complex Datatypes

Complex datatypes are object datatypes, and those available object datatypes vary depending on the database vendor. Relational databases generally provide more limited object structures in the form of object-relational attributes and functionality, as opposed to object functionality, which is really object storage and not object-based method processing because of the differences in design between relational and object databases. So in a relational database, a complex datatype is one that allows for insertion of objects into the storage areas of a relational database, including items such as binary multimedia objects, reference pointers, collection arrays, and even the capacity to create user-defined types with their own contained programming logic as object methods. These are some complex datatypes:

- **Binary Objects.** Purely binary objects were created in relational databases in order to help separate binary type data from regular relational database table row structures. A large object such as a graphic stored as a .BMP (BitMaP) file is much larger than the length of an average table row containing only strings and numbers, and so storage issues can become problematic trying to store a large map of binary numbers; a binary object stores the graphic in its native and uninterpreted form. Relational databases use many different types of underlying disk storage techniques in order to make the management of rows in tables more efficient. A typical row in a table will occupy part of a block in the operating system. Even the smallest of graphic objects used in website applications will fill a block with far fewer objects and also be spread out to fill more than one block if the object is large enough.

> Block sizes depend on the operating system and can be 2Kb, 4Kb, 8Kb, 16Kb, or even 32Kb in some cases.

- **Reference Pointers.** In the C programming language, a reference pointer is a variable containing an address on disk or in memory of whatever the programmer wants a program to point at. Some relational databases allow use of pointers where a pointer points to an object or file stored outside a table and outside the database, externally to the database; only the address of the externally stored object is stored in the table column. This minimizes adverse storage effects on relational tables but has a problem that the binary object will not be part of regular database backup procedures. So you may have to back up your binary storage areas separately, but binary objects are usually relatively static compared with simple strings, numbers, and dates.
- **Collection Arrays.** Some relational databases allow creation of what an object database calls a *collection*. A collection is a set of values repeated structurally (values are not necessarily the same), where the array is contained within another object and can only be referenced from that parent object as a child or sibling of that parent object. In

the case of a relational database, the containment factor is the collection being a column inside the table.

- **User-Defined Types**. Some relational databases allow programmable or even on-the-fly creation of user-defined types, which is like defining a table within a table. A user-defined type allows the creation of new types or new datatypes. In other words, columns can be created in tables where those columns have user-defined datatypes.

Specialized Datatypes

Specialized datatypes take into account datatypes that are intended for contained complex data objects where the datatype itself contains some accessible interpretable functionality stored within the object itself. A classic example of this is an XML document in which the data in the XML document is used to store both data and data describing the data (the metadata). Other types of specialized objects are used in Graphical Information Systems (GIS) and Medical Information Systems (MIS) in which annotations and extras can be manipulated on top of a basic image or binary structure.

2.2.1.2 Constraints

Relational databases allow what are called *constraints,* which constrain or restrict values that are allowed to be stored in table columns. Some relational databases allow the minimum of constraints necessary to define a database as being a relational database, whereas other relational databases allow more sophisticated constraints in addition to the basics. In general, constraints are used to restrict values in tables, make validation checks on one or more columns in a table, or even check values between columns between two different tables:

- **NOT NULL**. This is the simplest of columnar constraints, making sure that a value must always be entered into a column when a row is added or changed.
- **Validation Check**. A check constraint restricts the value to which a column can be set when a row is added or changed in a table. A check validation constraint can be as simple as making sure a column can be set to only M for Male or F for Female. Check constraints can

become fairly complex in some relational databases, even allowing inclusion of user-written functions running SQL scripting every time the constraint is checked.

- **Keys**. Key constraints include primary keys, foreign keys, and unique keys. Key constraints allow the checking and validation of unique values within the same table and values between columns between two different tables. Primary and foreign keys are the implementation of relationships between parent and child tables, where the primary key is placed on the parent table and the foreign key on the child table.

Some but not all relational databases allow constraints to be specified at both the column level or for an entire table as a whole, depending on the type of constraint.

2.2.2 Rows

Figure 2.9 shows the structure of columns applied to each row entry in a table. All you need to understand here is that a table can have multiple columns where that set of columns can have many rows created in the same table, and where data can subsequently be accessed according to the column structure of the table, row by row.

ISBN	AUTHOR	PUBLISHER	TITLE	GENRE	PRINTED
345333926	Larry Niven	Ballantine Books	Ringworld	Science Fiction	30-Nov-90
345336275	Isaac Azimov	Ballantine Books	Foundation	Science Fiction	31-Jul-86
345438353	James Blish	Ballantine Books	A Case of Conscience	Science Fiction	
553293362	Isaac Azimov	Bantam Books	Second Foundation	Science Fiction	
553278398	Isaac Azimov	Spectra	Prelude to Foundation	Science Fiction	
553293389	Isaac Azimov	Spectra	Foundation's Edge	Science Fiction	
553293370	Isaac Azimov	Spectra	Foundation and Empire	Science Fiction	
893402095	Isaac Azimov	L P Books	Foundation	Science Fiction	31-May-79
345323440	Larry Niven	Del Rey Books	Footfall	Science Fiction	31-Jul-96
345334787	Isaac Azimov	Del Rey Books	Foundation	Science Fiction	31-Dec-85
345308999	Isaac Azimov	Del Rey Books	Foundation	Science Fiction	28-Feb-83
5553673224	Isaac Azimov	Books on Tape	Foundation	Science Fiction	31-Jan-20
5557076654	Isaac Azimov	Books on Tape	Foundation	Science Fiction	31-Jan-51
246118318	Isaac Azimov	HarperCollins Publishers	Foundation	Science Fiction	28-Apr-83
449208133	Larry Niven	Fawcett Books	Lucifer's Hammer	Science Fiction	31-May-85
425130215	Kurt Vonnegut	Berkley Publishing Group	Hocus Pocus	Modern American	30-Nov-91

Figure 2.9 Rows repeat table column structure.

So far, this chapter has examined tables plus the columns and rows within those tables. The next step is to examine relationships between tables.

2.3 Relationships

Tables can have various types of relationships between them including one-to-one, one-to-many, one-to-zero or one, one-to-many or one, and many-to-many. The different types of inter-table relationships that can be formed between different tables can be best described by display in Entity Relationship Diagrams (ERDs).

> A table is often referred to as an *entity in an ERD,* and thus Entity Relationship Diagram or a diagram of related tables.

2.3.1 Representing Relationships in an ERD

An ERD displays tables and relationships between those tables; Figure 2.10 shows an ERD for tables in a schema containing published books, which is

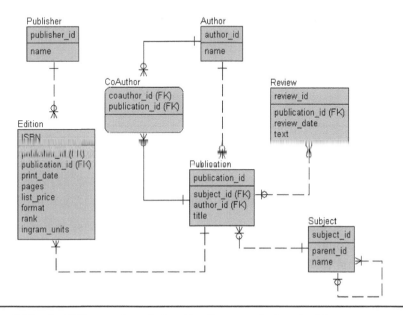

Figure 2.10   An ERD or entity relationship diagram of related tables.

a very basic structure of how books could be organized into a database for a book retailer, which could be used to represent some of the data for a corner book store.

2.3.1.1 Crows Foot

A crow's foot is used to describe the many side of a one-to-many or many-to-many relationship, as highlighted in Figure 2.11. A crow's foot looks quite literally like the imprint of a crow's foot in some mud with three splayed toes facing forwards and one facing backwards. Figure 2.11 shows a crow's foot between the AUTHOR and PUBLICATION tables, which indicates a one-to-many relationship between the AUTHOR and PUBLICATION tables.

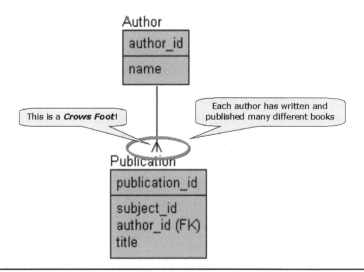

Figure 2.11   A crow's foot represents the many side of a one-to-many relationship in an ERD.

2.3.1.2 One-to-One Relationships

One-to-one relationships are rare in relational database models in comparison to one-to-many relationships, except for unusual database models. One-to-one relationships often occur where potentially NULL valued columns are removed from the parent table to save storage space or simply to decouple a subsection of data that only exists under specific circumstances. With the advent of cheap storage space, saving space has become

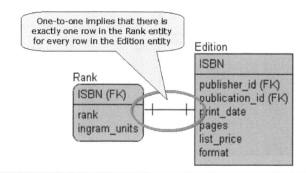

Figure 2.12   A one-to-one or zero relationship implies one or zero RANK for each EDITION.

less relevant. Using one-to-one related tables without good reason can be detrimental to performance, because SQL code joins get bigger and thus slower with more tables being joined, and bad database performance means slow applications and unhappy users.

Figure 2.12 shows a one-to-one or zero relationship between the EDITION and RANK tables such that for every EDITION entry, there may be a single RANK entry but there a RANK entry is required.

Figure 2.13 shows the equivalent of the one-to-one table structure representation from Figure 2.12, except that Figure 2.13 shows real data. For example, ISBNs 198711905 and 345308999 both have RANK and INGRAM_UNITS value entries and thus appear in the RANK table as unique rows. So Figure 2.13 shows clearly that there is exactly one row in the EDITION table for every row in the RANK table, and vice versa.

2.3.1.3 One-to-Many Relationships

One-to-many relationships are extremely common in the relational database model between tables. Figure 2.14 shows that an AUTHOR table row can have many publications, because an author can publish many books (PUBLICATION row entries).

Figure 2.15 shows a data diagram with authors on the right of the diagram and their respective publications on the left, in a one-to-many relationship. One author has two titles, another author has five titles, a third author has three titles, two authors have one title each, and a further two authors have nothing published at all in this example (Orson Scott Card and Jerry Pournelle).

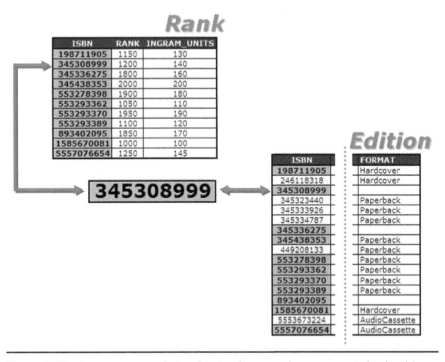

Figure 2.13 A one-to-one relationship implies exactly one entry in both tables.

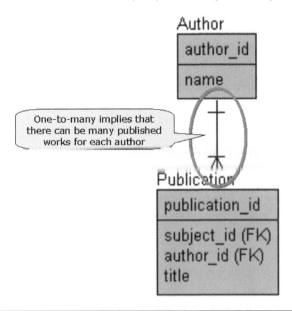

Figure 2.14 One-to-many implies one entry to many entries between two tables.

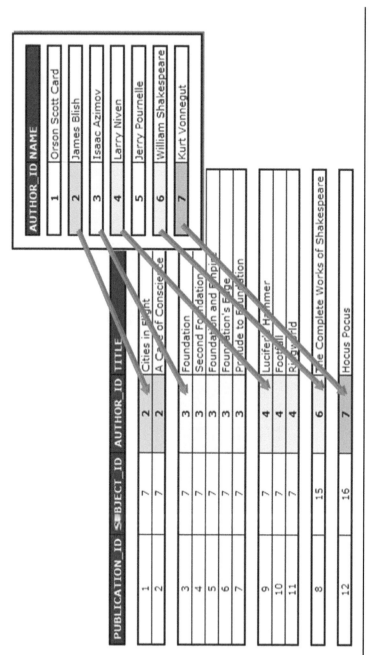

Figure 2.15 One-to-many implies one entry to many entries between two tables.

2.3.1.4 Many-to-Many Relationships

A many-to-many relationship means that for every one row in one table there are many possible rows in another related table, and vice versa (for both tables). A frequently used example of a many-to-many relationship is many students enrolled in many courses at a university. The implication is that every student is registered for many courses and every course has many students registered for it, which results in a many-to-many relationship between students and courses. If an application or end user needs to find an individual course taken by an individual student, then a uniquely identifying table is required.

> Many-to-many join resolution tables have many different names, including *linking table* and *associative table*.

In Figure 2.16, from left to right, the many-to-many relationship between PUBLISHER and PUBLICATION tables is resolved into the EDITION table.

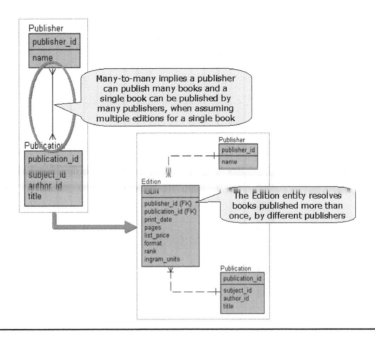

Figure 2.16   Resolving a many-to-many relationship with a new table.

A publisher can publish many publications, and a single publication can be published by many publishers. Not only can a single publication be reprinted, but other types of media such as an audio version can also be produced, and those different versions can be produced by different publishers as well; specialized publishers usually produce audio versions of books regardless if by the author or an actor. The purpose of the EDITION table is to provide a way for each individual reprint and audio edition to be uniquely accessible in the database.

In Figure 2.17, there are seven different editions of the publication Foundation, books written by a science fiction author called Isaac Azimov. Isaac Azimov wrote a lot of books for decades and is an extremely popular science fiction author. The book titled Foundation was written many years ago and has been in print ever since it was first published and has also been reprinted many times.

Searching for this particular publication without the ISBN unique for each edition would always find seven editions in the data, as shown in Figure 2.17. If only one of the *Books On Tape* editions was required for a query, returning seven rows rather than only one could cause some confusion, and so a many-to-many join resolution table in the form of the EDITION table is needed to find unique editions among the seven different versions of the same publication.

TITLE	PUBLISHER	ISBN	PRINTED
Cities in Flight	Overlook Press	1585670081	
A Case of Conscience	Ballantine Books	345438353	
Foundation	HarperCollins Publishe	246118318	28-Apr
Foundation	Books on Tape	5553673224	31-
Foundation	Books on Tape	5557070054	31-Jan-51
Foundation	Del Rey Books	945994707	31-Dec-05
Foundation	Del Rey Books	345308999	28-Feb-83
Foundation	L P Books	893402095	31-May-79
Foundation	Ballantine Books	345336275	31-Jul-86
Second Foundation	Bantam Books	553293362	
Foundation and Empire	Spectra	553293370	
Foundation's Edge	Spectra	553293389	
Prelude to Foundation	Spectra	553278398	
Lucifer's Hammer	Fawcett Books	449208133	31-May-85
Footfall	Del Rey Books	345323440	31-Jul-96
Ringworld	Ballantine Books	345333926	30-Nov-90

Each edition is uniquely identified by an ISBN – unique to each new edition of the same title

Figure 2.17   Resolving a many-to-many relationship into a new table.

2.3.1.5 Zero, One, or Many Relationships

Relationships between tables can be zero, one, or many, where zero implies that the row does not have to exist in the target table, one implies that it can exist (if with zero), and one implies it must exist (if without zero); many simply implies many. The left side of Figure 2.18 shows a one-to-zero or exactly-one relationship between the RANK and EDITION tables. This implies that an EDITION row does not have to have a related RANK row entry, but because the zero is pointing at the RANK table then the same is not the case in reverse. In other words, for every RANK entry there must be exactly one row in the EDITION table. Therefore, individual editions of books do not have to be ranked, but a ranking requires a book edition to rank. In other words, it is not possible to rank a book that does not exist, but a new book does not have to have a rank yet.

Similarly, on the right side of Figure 2.18, a publisher can be a publisher even if that publisher currently has no books published. If a publishing company no longer exists but the books it published are still in print as used books, then they still exist as publications of the work.

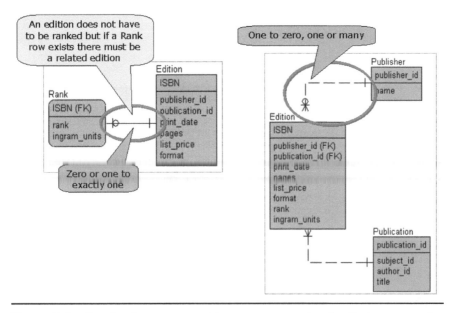

Figure 2.18   One implies a row must be present. zero implies that a row can be present.

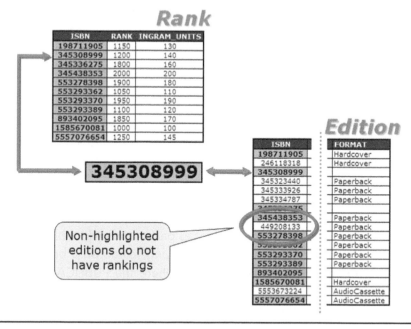

Figure 2.19   A one-to-one or zero relationship.

Figure 2.19 shows the equivalent of the one-to-one table structure representation using similar data to that in Figure 2.13, except that in Figure 2.19 not every edition has a rank (some editions have no rank entry). ISBNs 198711905 and 345308999 both have RANK and INGRAM_UNITS value entries and thus appear in the RANK table as unique rows. On the contrary, the edition with ISBN 246118318 does not have any information with respect to rank and Ingram unit values, and thus RANK and INGRAM_ UNITS column values would be NULL valued for this edition of this book. Thus the relationship between EDITION and RANK tables in Figure 2.19 is one-to-one or zero.

2.3.1.6 Identifying and Non-Identifying Relationships

Figure 2.20 shows identifying relationships, non-identifying relationships and dependent tables—all can be described as follows:

- **Identifying Relationship**. The child table is partially identified by the parent table, and thus partially dependent on the parent table. The parent table primary key is included in the primary key of the child table as shown in Figure 2.20, where the COAUTHOR table includes both the AUTHOR and PUBLICATION primary keys as part of the COAUTHOR primary key, or in this case as the complete composite of the two parent table columns.

- o **Dependent Entity or Table.** The COAUTHOR table is dependent on the AUTHOR and PUBLICATION tables, and so a dependent table exists for a table with an identifying relationship to a parent table.
- o **Non-Dependent Entity or Table.** This is the opposite of a dependent table.
- **Non-Identifying Relationship.** The child table is not dependent on the parent table such that the child table includes the parent table primary key as a foreign key, but not as part of the child table's primary key. Figure 2.20 shows a non-identifying relationship between the AUTHOR and PUBLICATION tables where the PUBLICATION table contains the AUTHOR_ID primary key column from the AUTHOR table; however, the AUTHOR_ID column is not part of the primary key in the PUBLICATION table.

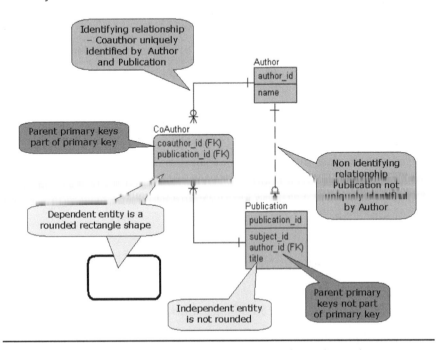

Figure 2.20 Identifying, non-identifying, and dependent relationships.

2.3.2 Keys to Enforce Referential Integrity

Relational databases use the terms *key* and *index* to indicate similar concepts. An index is a copy of a small number of columns (preferably one column) from a table and is structured in a specific format such as a BTree index. An index can be created on any column in a table. A key, on the other hand, is more of a concept than a physical thing because a key is also an index, but in a relational database a key is a term used to describe the columns that link tables together in order to form relationships, such as a one-to-many relationship between two tables. There are two basic types of keys: (1) a primary key, and (2) a foreign key.

2.3.2.1 Primary Key

A primary key is used to identify the values that most distinctly define the data in a table, uniquely identifying each row in a table. Figure 2.21 shows primary key columns of AUTHOR_ID for the AUTHOR table and PUBLICATION_ID for the PUBLICATION table, each being primary key columns for the two respective tables. So each author is identified by a single AUTHOR_ID and each publication by one PUBLICATION_ID, and both these keys will be used by other tables to link back to the parent table containing the primary key values.

A table can contain only one primary key, because the primary key uniquely identifies each row in a table in relation to itself in addition to all other tables in a relational data model. You cannot identify related rows with more than one primary key in the same table, which is not therefore allowed, otherwise a child row could have multiple parent rows.

Unique Key

A primary key is a type of unique key because it identifies a row in a table uniquely to other tables as well as the table the primary key is on; however, you can also have a unique key that is unique that is not linked to other tables. Like a primary key, a unique key is created on a column containing only unique values throughout an entire table. For example, if you look back at Figure 2.21, you can see that authors are uniquely identified by an integer contained in the AUTHOR_ID column, but it would still make sense to set the name of the author as a unique key so that you do not create an

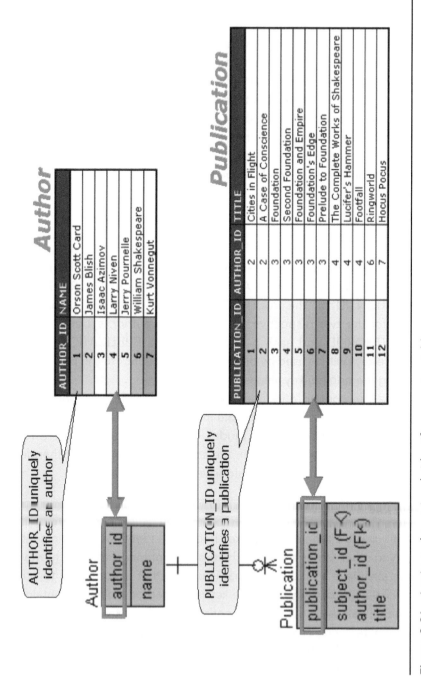

Author

AUTHOR_ID	NAME
1	Orson Scott Card
2	James Blish
3	Isaac Azimov
4	Larry Niven
5	Jerry Pournelle
6	William Shakespeare
7	Kurt Vonnegut

Publication

PUBLICATION_ID	AUTHOR_ID	TITLE
1	2	Cities in Flight
2	2	A Case of Conscience
3	3	Foundation
4	3	Second Foundation
5	3	Foundation and Empire
6	3	Foundation's Edge
7	3	Prelude to Foundation
8	4	The Complete Works of Shakespeare
9	4	Lucifer's Hammer
10	4	Footfall
11	6	Ringworld
12	7	Hocus Pocus

AUTHOR_ID uniquely identifies an author

Author
- author id
- name

PUBLICATION_ID uniquely identifies a publication

Publication
- publication_id
- subject_id (F◇)
- author_id (FK)
- title

Figure 2.21 A primary key uniquely identifies a row in a table.

author more than once. Also an integer is used in the AUTHOR_ID column, replacing the name of the author as the primary key of the AUTHOR table as an integer surrogate key (replacement key).

Surrogate Key

You may be wondering why integers are used as primary keys in Figure 2.15, Figure 2.19, and Figure 2.21. The reason is that the tables contain generated surrogate (replacement) integer values that are used as primary keys, replacing the unique names of items such as the name of an author or a publication. For example, the AUTHOR_ID column in the AUTHOR table is a surrogate primary key as a replacement or surrogate for creating the primary on the AUTHOR table NAME column, NAME being the full name of the author. It is very unlikely that there will be two authors with the same name but it can happen.

> A surrogate key is usually an integer auto counter or sequence, which replaces the natural key on the name of an item. A natural key is known as a natural key because it indexes the potentially unique name of an item such as an author's name or the title of a book. In addition, a natural key is sometimes called a business key. In the case of something like a song title, that song titles are not copyrightable and so names cannot always be assumed to be unique, because others may reuse a song title over and over again.

Surrogate keys are also used as integers because integers make for faster key searches; number values are generally shorter in length than strings; however, storage space is not really an issue in modern times because storage is now cheap. On the contrary, keys have specialized structures, and integers have only ten different digits in each character position (strings have all possible alphanumeric characters), so integer keys tend to result in much faster seek times because of the way indexes are structured.

> Another less obvious reason for the use of surrogate keys in a relational database is because they create a better look-and-feel to overlaying object methodology applications written in programming languages like Java.

As an example of a surrogate primary key, the AUTHOR table could be created with a simple script such as the following:

```
CREATE TABLE Author
(
    author_id INTEGER NOT NULL,
    name VARCHAR(32) NULL,
    PRIMARY KEY (author_id),
    UNIQUE (name)
);
```

In the script above, the primary key is set to the AUTHOR_ID column, and the name of the author is set to be unique to ensure that the same author is not added twice, or that two authors do not use the same pseudonym, because in this particular case of books, two authors cannot have the same name. The primary key will be used for referencing other related tables, and the unique name key will not.

2.3.2.2 Foreign Key

Foreign keys are the copies of primary keys added to child tables in order to form a link between a parent table with a primary key and a child table containing a copy of the parent table's primary key, stored in the related child table as a foreign key.

> In the relational data model a parent table can contain more than one child table, and a child table can have more than one parent table, such as the EDITION and CHILD_AUTHOR tables; a table can contain more than one foreign key and point at multiple parent tables.

In relational database terminology, the link between a primary and foreign key forms a relationship between two relations, where the integrity between two tables is enforced by the existence of the primary key in the parent table, and the foreign key in the child table must exist in the parent table as a primary key value. The result is that a row in a table using a foreign key must exist as a primary key value in a row of the parent table, which ensures that the reference values between the two tables are valid.

The only exception to this rule is for a non-identifying relationship, in which a foreign key can be null.

> A relation is synonymous with a table and an entity—
> they all mean the same thing.

So a foreign key defines a reference for each row in the child table, referencing back to the primary key in the parent table. Figure 2.22 shows that the PUBLICATION table has a foreign key called AUTHOR_ID (FK). The result is that each row in the PUBLICATION table has a copy of the parent table's AUTHOR_ID column value (its primary key value) in the

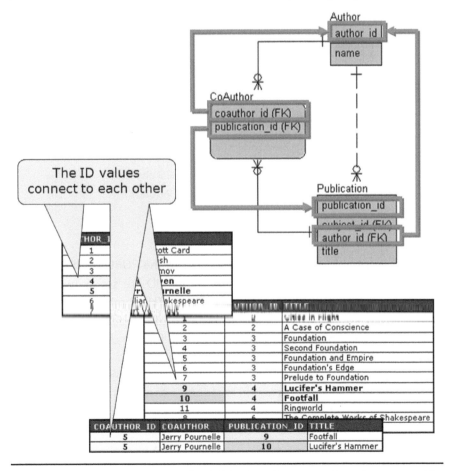

Figure 2.22 A foreign key is used to link back to the primary key of a parent table.

AUTHOR_ID foreign key column on the PUBLICATION table. In other words, an author can have many books published and available for sale at once. Similarly, in Figure 2.22 the COAUTHOR table has a primary key made up of two columns, which is comprised by the combination or composite of a two foreign key relationship back to both the AUTHOR table and the PUBLICATION table.

> A key consisting of more than one column on the same table is known as a *composite key*.

The PUBLICATION table could be created with a simple script such as the following:

```
CREATE TABLE Publication
(
    publication_id INTEGER NOT NULL,
    subject_id INTEGER NOT NULL,
    author_id INTEGER NOT NULL,
    title VARCHAR(64) NULL,
    PRIMARY KEY (publication_id),
    FOREIGN KEY (subject_id) REFERENCES Subject,
    FOREIGN KEY (author_id) REFERENCES Author,
    UNIQUE (title)
);
```

In the script above, the primary key is set to the PUBLICATION_ID column. The columns SUBJECT_ID and AUTHOR_ID are set as two foreign key reference columns to the SUBJECT and AUTHOR tables, respectively. A unique key constraint is applied to the title of the publication to make sure that two authors do not use the same title for two different books.

> In the world of book publishing using the same title, or even a similar title for a book, is generally regarded as a copyright infringement, and so book titles have to be unique. As already stated, in the world of music, song titles cannot be copyrighted because otherwise songwriters would have run out of titles decades ago. In the world of books the titles and authors are generally different.

So remember that a primary key uniquely identifies each row in a table, and a foreign key is a copy of the primary key copied from a parent table, establishing and enforcing a relationship between parent and child tables. A unique key simply ensures the uniqueness of a value within a table, and a surrogate key replaces a primary key with a more efficient and definitely unique value.

2.3.2.3 Referential Integrity

Referential integrity functions just as its name states—it ensures the integrity of referential relationships between tables as defined by primary and foreign keys. In a relationship between two tables, one table has a primary key and the other a foreign key, and the primary key uniquely identifies each row in the first table. In other words, there can be only one row in the first table with the same primary key value. The foreign key is placed into the second table in the relationship such that the foreign key contains a copy of the primary key value from the row in the related table.

So what is referential integrity? The fact that, as already stated in the above paragraph, referential integrity ensures the integrity of relationships between primary and foreign key values in related tables does not really say all that much. Most relational database engines use what are often called *constraints*—primary and foreign keys are both constraints. A constraint is a piece of metadata defined for a table defining restrictions on values. A primary key constraint forces the primary key column to be unique, and a primary key constraint is also forced to make checks against any foreign key constraints referenced back to that primary key constraint. Referencing or referential foreign key constraints can be in any table, including the same table as the primary key constrained column referenced by the foreign key (a self join). A foreign key constraint uses its reference to refer back to a referenced table, containing the primary key constraint in order to ensure that the two values in the primary key column and foreign key column match.

In modern relational databases, primary and foreign keys automatically verify against each other. Primary and foreign key references are the connections establishing and enforcing referential integrity between tables and thus the integrity and validity of data. There are some specific circumstances to consider in terms of how referential integrity is enforced:

> A primary key table is assumed to be a parent table
> and a foreign key table a child table.

- When adding a new row to a child table, if a foreign key value is entered, it must exist in the related primary key column of the parent table.

> Foreign key columns can contain NULL values. Primary key column values can never contain NULL values because they are required to be unique. NULL foreign keys create a non-identifying relationship with a parent table's primary key, because the child row is not strictly identified by the parent table's primary key (the foreign key value does not have to exist). A non-NULL foreign key partially identifies the child table row and can be a part of a composite primary key in the child table.

- When changing a row in a parent table, if the primary key is changed, then the change must be cascaded to all foreign key valued rows in any related child tables. Otherwise the change to the parent table must be prohibited.

> The term *cascade* implies that changes to data in parent tables are automatically propagated to all child tables containing foreign key column copies of a primary key, copied from a parent table.

- When changing a row in a child table, a change to a foreign key requires that a related primary key must be checked for existence, or the primary must be changed first. If a foreign key is changed to NULL, then no primary key is required. If the foreign key is changed to a non-NULL value, then the foreign key value must exist as a primary key value in the related parent table again.
- When deleting a parent table row, then related foreign key rows in child tables must either be cascade deleted automatically or deleted from child tables first.

Figure 2.23 shows some data, and you can do the following exercise with that data to better understand referential integrity with primary and foreign keys:

BAND NAME	TRACK	DESCRIPTION
Nirvana	Come As You Are	Bass reverb
Greetings From Limbo	The Right Line	Country groove
Pearl Jam	Fatal	Deadly
Foo Fighters		
Greetings From Limbo	Ashes	Heavy
Red Hot Chili Peppers	My Friends	Hmmm
Red Hot Chili Peppers	Otherside	Hmmm again
Red Hot Chili Peppers	Californication	Hot and dry
Pearl Jam	Immortality	Just imagine
Nirvana	About A Girl	Lots of lovely bass
Red Hot Chili Peppers	Suck My Kiss	No thanks
Pearl Jam	Around The Bend	Nuts!
Red Hot Chili Peppers	Universally Speaking	OK
Nirvana	The Man Who Sold The World	Sell out!
Stone Temple Pilots		
Greetings From Limbo	Greetings From Limbo	The Wizard of Oz
Red Hot Chili Peppers	Under the Bridge	Where's that confounded bridge?
Soundgarden		
Nirvana	Polly	Who's that?

Figure 2.23   Band names, tracks, and silly descriptions.

1. Create two related tables linked by a one-to-many relationship.
2. Assign a primary key column to each table.
3. Assign a foreign key column to one table, which links to a primary key in the other table.

So you are asked for two tables using the three columns of data as shown in Figure 2.23. One table will have one column and the other table two columns, because one band has many tracks, which is the obvious one-to-many relationship; and it also removes the duplications of the names of each band even though the data is inconveniently and deliberately unsorted. These are the steps you can take to solve this problem without using any complicated theory, but simply by knowing a little about modern music:

1. The first column contains the names of numerous different bands (musical groups), and the second column contains a track or the name of a song. Typically, different bands or musical groups create many tracks, and so a one-to-many relationship exists between the names of bands and the track names.
2. Band names in the first column are duplicated, and track names and descriptions in the second and third columns are not duplicated; this supports the solution already derived in 1 above.

3. Band names are the only duplicated values, so they make up the table on the parent side of the one-to-many relationship, whereas the other two columns contain no duplicates and thus make up the table on the child side of the relationship.
4. The track name must identify the track uniquely, and the description is irrelevant to the relationship between bands and tracks.

Figure 2.24 shows three viable solutions, with option 3 being the better of all of the three options because surrogate keys are used for the primary and foreign keys. This is because song titles are not copyrightable and can thus be re-used; do a Google search for the song title She, as in "song title She", and you will find a few. Option 2 is better than option 1, because in option 2 the one-to-many relationship is a non-identifying relationship, where the primary key on the TRACK table is not a composite key (composite keys are larger and more complicated and thus slower to change and read).

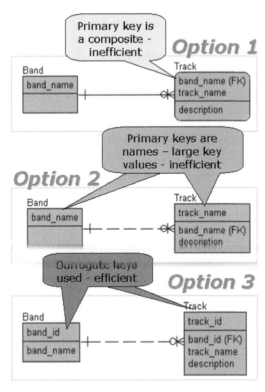

Figure 2.24   Band names, tracks and silly descriptions represented in various ERDs.

2.4 Indexes

Indexes are not a logical part of the relational database model, but they are part of the physical relational database model; however, indexes are so important to performance and overall database usability that they have to be discussed briefly in a book on what is mostly logical data modeling. It is important to understand the fundamentals of indexes and some basic different types in order to get a brief understanding as to why exactly indexing is so important for relational databases in general.

2.4.1 What is an Index?

An index is usually and preferably a copy of a very small section of a table, such as a single short-length column like an integer or a fixed-length string under five characters. An index physically copies one or more columns to be indexed into a separate area of disk other than that of the table, and the table is accessed precisely from the index using a direct address on disk. When a table is accessed, a process often called an *optimizer* decides whether to access the table alone, scanning all the rows in the table, or if it is faster to read the much smaller index in conjunction with a very small section of the table.

> All relational databases have some type of SQL execution optimization process—it is usually called the optimizer.

An index essentially behaves like an index in the back of a book or the table of contents at the front of a book. When searching for details on a specific topic, it is much easier to find the term in the index or table of contents first, and then using a page reference number to find the information within the pages of the text. Reading the entire book every time one wants to find a definition for a single term would be far too time consuming to be useful, probably making the book completely useless as a reference. Most technical books are used as reference guides in one form or another. An index in a relational database performs the same function as a person using the table of contents at the front of a book or the index at the back of a book to find something quickly.

Things to be avoided when indexing are creation of too many indexes, placing too many columns into individual indexes, and over usage of exotic indexes. Too many indexes on a table can result in slower database response time because every change to a table updates every index attached to it in addition to the table; the more indexes created for a table the more physical changes are required. Indexing too many columns not only makes the use of the indexes by queries more complex but also makes the indexes larger physically and thus longer to read and more difficult to build into specialized index structures; an index must be relatively very much smaller than a table and should be created on as few columns as possible from that individual table. Exotic indexes such as bitmaps and clusters have their place, but do not overuse them because there can be unexpected side effects.

2.4.2 Alternate Indexing

Alternate indexing comes from the terms *alternate index, secondary index,* or *tertiary index.* Specific use of terminology depends on the database in use. These terms all mean the same thing, but where an alternate index is an alternative and is additional to the principal relational structure organized by primary and foreign key indexes, which enforce business rules between tables for referential integrity.

2.4.2.1 Foreign Key Indexing

Relationships between tables, such as that between the AUTHOR and PUBLICATION tables as shown in Figure 2.21, can allow the foreign key in the child table not only to be duplicated (one-to-many), but also to be NULL valued in the child table (one-to-zero, one or many). So in Figure 2.21, each author can have multiple publications, or an author does not have to have any publications at all. Indexes must be created on those foreign key columns manually because foreign keys are allowed to be NULL valued and do not have to be unique.

> Relational databases automatically create internal unique indexes on primary keys because a primary key must be unique, in that every time a row is added to the table, all other rows must be checked against for the uniqueness of the newly added row—also it is much faster to check against an index rather than read the entire table.

Commands similar to the following commands could be used to create indexes on foreign key columns, for the CREATE TABLE command on the PUBLICATION table shown previously in this chapter:

```
CREATE INDEX XFK_P_Author ON Publication(author_id);
CREATE INDEX XFK_P_Publisher ON Publication(subject_id);
```

2.4.3 Types of Indexes

It is important to have a brief understanding of different types of indexing available in relational databases. Smaller-scale database tools such Microsoft Access® (MSAccess) might offer little or no variation on index types allowed (usually BTree type indexing). On the other hand, other more sophisticated databases allow for a few different types of indexes. Some of the different types of indexes available are as follows:

- **BTree Index**. BTree means *balanced tree* or sometimes *binary tree*, and if drawn out on a piece of paper, a BTree index looks like an upside-down tree. A balanced tree BTree index consists of a root node, branch nodes, and leaf nodes, where leaf nodes contain the indexed column values. Some BTree construction and searching methods in some databases are highly efficient for both reading and changing of data, automatically changing the structure of the BTree index without any overflow—mostly. Figure 2.25 shows an example picture of what a typical relational database BTree index might look like.

Overflow is usually but not always bad for indexing because changes are placed outside of the optimized index structure and subsequent searches for overflow values search storage outside the initially constructed index, which is extremely inefficient. BTree indexes do not exactly overflow, even in extreme circumstances.

A BTree index can extend to more than three levels in addition to a single root node, a single branch layer, and single leaf layer. This can occur with a really large index when the root or a branch node block runs out of space, extending a specific branch or the root node, creating a branch linked from the original root or branch node, respectively. In this type of situation, a BTree can be split into as many as four or five layers, where a search for a specific index value

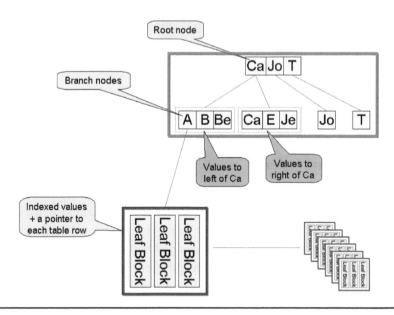

Figure 2.25   A BTree index.

could take more than the usual three hits of root, branch, and leaf, depending on how many additional layers there are. This is a form of overflow, but it is logical rather than physical disk location chains, and rebuilding a BTree index altogether will recreate the index again in its balanced three-layer format anyway.

- **Bitmap Index**. Figure 2.26 shows a picture of a bitmap index where a bitmap index contains binary representations for each row using 0s and 1s. Bitmap indexes are often misused and are extremely vulnerable to overflow even after a low percentage of all rows in a table are changed; the index deteriorates rapidly. A bitmap index's overflow values cannot be slotted into the existing bitmap index structure, as can be done when updating a BTree index. Figure 2.26 shows a graphical type structure of the internal machinations of a bitmap index where two bitmaps are created for two values of M for Male and F for Female. So when M is encountered, then the M bitmap is set to 1 and the F bitmap is set to 0. Bitmap indexes are disappointing even in environments where they are supposedly highly beneficial, such as data warehouse databases, because even with a very small ratio of different values, even small numbers of updates to values without a full rebuild on bitmap indexes can cause a serious degradation in performance.

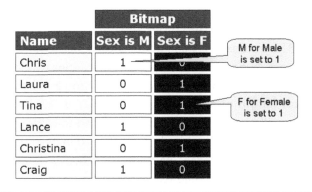

Figure 2.26   A bitmap index.

> In modern data warehouses indexes have been discarded altogether,
> and index types such as bitmaps are more of an approach to get
> around the restrictions that relational database modeling place
> on a data warehouse's need to just read everything.

- **ISAM Index**. ISAM means Indexed Sequential Access Method and uses a simple structure with a list of row numbers. ISAM indexes have been used in MySQL and were used in Ingres in the past—a long time in the past. They are best used for static data because their internal list structure prohibits easy changes, which makes them extremely vulnerable to index overflow and performance problems.
- **Hash Table**. A hash table is a copy of data but rearranged into a different and more efficiently accessed order, depending on the result of a hashing algorithm as applied to each hashed index value. A hashing algorithm can generate a smooth distribution of values and takes, for instance a string, and creates a number from that string. The number created by a specific string will always be the same and is thus placed in a position in an index, sorted based on the hash calculated value. Hash indexes can be highly efficient for read access but are best avoided when subjected to any kind of data changes. Hash table indexes overflow regardless, and regeneration of hash indexes is the norm when changes are made to data. Hashing algorithms are commonly used in indexes where the datasets do not have to be maintained in real time.

- **Index Organized Table**. An Index Organized table, or IOT, builds an entire table into the sorted order and structure of an index, typically using a BTree index. IOTs can actually work fairly well in many types of databases, but one has to remember that index row length is much longer than normal, as index leaf blocks contain all columns in the entire row length of a table. Also if the IOT is not read in indexed order, then all rows in the table are read, and thus the index is pointless because index and table data is scanned in its entirety. IOTs can be useful, but in databases with constant heavy database changes involving updates and deletes they can become disorganized and poorly performing much quicker than a regular BTree index, simply because each index is much bigger.

> An IOT is known as an index organized table in Oracle Database and a clustered index in SQL Server Database. Clusters in Oracle Database are similar but don not copy all the columns from a table, only the most likely used columns.

2.4.4 Different Ways to Build Indexes

Indexes can usually be built in various different ways in order to accommodate the different ways in which they might be used. Once again, some relational databases allow all of the following options, some allow some of these options, and some allow none:

- **Ascending or Descending Index**. An index can be built sorted in ascending order such as A, B, C or also in descending order as in the reverse sequence: C, B, A.
- **Unique Index**. An index can be unique, which means it cannot contain any duplicate values, where querying a duplicated value simply returns more than one row. It is normal to create both unique indexes and non-unique indexes on the same table; a non-unique index contains duplicated or repeated values for the index in the table.
- **Composite Index**. Indexes can be built on more than a single column and are known as *composite column indexes, multiple column indexes,* or just *composite indexes.* The most efficient type of index is a single-column index containing an integer, because they are simple

and have few different values in each byte (0-9). Composite indexes are not always the best performing choice because they can be larger and might have strings in them.

- **Compressed Indexes**. Some databases allow compression of composite indexes where repeated prefix values are indexed within the index, removing duplications within prefixed indexed columns. In other words, a composite index containing three columns can be accessed using only something like the second and third columns because they are not dependent on the first column.

- **Reverse Key Indexes**. This is an unusual one, and only one database that I know of allows building of indexes such that indexed column values are stored as reverse strings. When adding huge numbers of rows at once to the same index in a very busy database, adding sequential index values (not reversed) adds lots of rows all at once to the same physical space (block) in the index, such as in data warehouse that adds huge quantities of data on a regular basis.

> A *block* is a term used to describe a chunk of space on disk used by the operating system (Windows, Linux®, or UNIX®), in order to manage disk space. Some databases can also manage disk space at the block level as a multiple of blocks managed by the underlying operating system.

The result is what some relational databases call *locking* and other relational databases call *hot blocking*, which is a kind of gridlock where very little gets done. Reverse keys can help to make the index values not be sequential in terms of where they are physically written to disk because the values will be placed into a pseudo-random order on disk, and thus in separate index blocks, thereby reducing competition for the same block. The result is less locking, less hot blocking, no gridlock, and thus much better performance.

2.5 Specialized Objects

So far in this chapter topics covered are tables, the relationship between those tables, and indexes attached to tables. You should understand the basic structure of a table and also that the relationships between tables are determined by primary keys in parent tables linked to foreign keys in child tables; foreign keys are copies of primary key column values from parent tables. Indexing is important to understand, not directly only from a modeling perspective but for two other reasons as well: (1) indexes are used to superimpose a different order on top of the order created by the natural way that data is added to a database by applications (daily), and (2) the very structure of the relationships between tables, imposed by primary and foreign keys, does impose a physical order on the way in which data is added to a database.

Other than all these wonderful indexing options, there are still even further possibilities within relational databases that some databases allow and some do not. It is important to know that specialized objects exist as options for expansion to a relational database model, as extensions to both the underlying physical structure of a database, as well as the overlying logical structure (the tables and indexes):

- **Views**. A view is a query definition that does not store any data, but its query is executed automatically whenever the view is called in a query. So every execution against a view will execute the query contained within the view against all underlying tables, and the danger with using views is filtering a query against a view, expecting to read a very small portion of a very large table, but the entire table is often read because the view is filtered and not the table. Any filtering should be done within the view, because any filtering against the view itself is applied after the query in the view has completed execution. Views are typically useful for speeding up the development process, but in the long run they can completely kill database performance. The secret with views is not to overuse them and most especially do not layer them (call one view from another from another in a hierarchy), because only the most sophisticated databases can execute filters applied in views onto underlying tables when a view is read, and a hierarchical structure of views deep enough will be beyond the capabilities of a database optimizer.
- **Materialized Views**. Materialized views are available in some very large-capacity type relational databases. A materialized view materializes underlying physical data by making a physical copy (or addressed copy) of data from tables. So unlike a view as described in the previous bullet point, when a query is executed against a materialized view, then

the materialized view is physically accessed rather than the underlying tables. The objective is to free the underlying tables for other uses, by creating two separate physical copies. Materialized views are often used to aggregate large data sets down to smaller sized data sets, in data warehouses and data marts. The biggest potential problem with materialized views is how often and how quickly they are refreshed and brought up to date with any changes to their underlying tables. Another attribute of materialized views is the ability of some database engines to allow a query directed at an underlying table to be automatically redirected to a physically much smaller materialized view. This is called *automated query rewrite.* What this means is that queries can be automatically rewritten by the query optimizer if the query rewrite can help to increase query performance.

- **Clusters**. Clusters are used in very few databases and have been somewhat superseded by materialized views. In the past, clusters were used to pre-create physical copies of a subset of columns of heavily accessed tables, especially tables accessed in SQL joins. Unlike materialized views clusters will not allow automatic refresh and are normally manually maintained.

The words *cluster, clustered,* and *clustering* are used for many different things in the database world. On the physical level a cluster is often a cluster of machines that store the same or different copies of data, and then execute insertions and queries in parallel (BigData and HDFS/Hadoop). Other clustering is Oracle® Real Application Clusters, which clusters or groups the CPU and memory power but shares the storage layer between those clustered nodes of machines, effectively severely limiting the ability to parallel process. Another use of the word clustering is as above in the form of an Oracle clustered table that creates a copy of a small number highly used columns in a table; SQL Server, on the other hand, uses the term clustered index to describe an IOT or index organized table (IOTs are Oracle), which is a table built with all columns in the sequence and structure of a BTree index. So it is easy to confuse terms in the database world, because reuse by different vendors and technologies is not always consistent.

- **Sequences and Auto Counters**. An auto counter column is a special functionally embedded datatype (sometimes called a *non-static internal function*), which allows automated generation of sequential number values, and thus the term *sequence.* Typically, auto counters are used for primary key surrogate key generation on insertion of new rows into a table.

> Oracle calls a sequence counter and sequence and SQL Server plus Microsoft Access call the same thing an auto-counter.

- **Partitioning and Parallel Processing**. Some databases allow physical splitting of tables into separate partitions, including parallel processing on multiple partitions and individual operations on individual partitions. One particularly efficient aspect of partitioning is something known as *partition pruning*, where a query reading a table can read fewer than all the partitions making up a table, perhaps even an individual partition. Partitioning has come into very prevalent use in data warehouses, both those built in relational database engines such as Oracle and SQL Server, in addition to modern data warehouse clustered and MPP (Massively Parallel Processing Platforms). Also, partitioning can be horizontal (splits rows) and vertical (splits columns), some database engines do both horizontal and vertical partitioning at the same time; most data warehouses platform do both, Oracle allows only horizontal, and SQL Server accommodates both.

2.6 Conclusion

This chapter covered:

- Building tables containing columns, datatypes, and constraints
- The different types of relationships between tables
- Defining relationships between tables with primary and foreign keys
- The types and uses of indexes
- The types and uses of specialized objects such as views, materialized views, auto counters, and partitions

The next chapter will examine the very heart of the relational database model by examining the process of normalization through the application of normal forms.

Chapter 3

Intuitive Relational Data Modeling and Normalization

There are two rules in life. Rule #1: Don't sweat the small stuff.
Rule #2: Everything is small stuff.[*]

—Richard Carlson

Life is as complicated as we make it—normalization
can be made the same sometimes.

This chapter examines the detail of the normalization process, in which normalization is the sequence of steps by which a relational database model is both created and improved upon. This sequence of steps involved in the normalization process is called *normal forms*, which is applied to a data model as a step-by-step process.

Previous chapters have examined database evolution and the pieces that make up the separate elements of database model design. This chapter expands particularly on the previous chapter (The Pieces of the Relational Database Model), using the terminology covered in the previous

---

* http://quotetab.com/quotes/by-finn-taylor#sxb5i4R7IUPtiFJO.97

chapter, explaining how to build a relational database model with things like tables, columns, and keys.

> Normalization can be described as being one of introduction of granularity, removal of duplication, minimizing of redundancy, or also the introduction of tables that place data into a more detailed and more easily accessible state.

The real purpose of this chapter is two-fold: (1) to describe the accepted method of relational database design in the form of normalization using normal forms, and (2) to describe my personal approach to building databases, which is not normalization but more of an intuitive approach using not only some parts of normalization, but also practical knowledge of the way in which a business works. You will begin by reading the formal definitions of normalization and normal forms and then dive straight into my intuitive approach, all demonstrated by example. Finally, toward the middle of this chapter, you will return to the accepted method of normalization and normal forms. The objective is to make the learning curve easier so that you have an understanding of what you are actually doing from a business perspective when you apply normal forms to normalize tables. At that stage, you can then choose how you will create relational database models for yourself; I find a mixture of both methods works best.

> An intuitive method of relational database model design is not normalization and normal forms, and it does not intend to borrow or steal from accepted practice. Intuitively I tend to focus on the results of what normalization produces rather than try to generically reach the same result using an abstracted only mathematical approach that is independent of the function of the business being modeled.

This chapter covers:

- Defining normalization and normal forms
- An intuitive and business-oriented method of building relational database models
- Anomalies and determinants
- What are 1st, 2nd, 3rd, Boyce-Codd, 4th, 5th, and Domain Key normal forms?
- Applying normalization and normal forms by example

3.1 Normalization and Normal Forms

It is sensible to begin with the definitions of normalization and normal forms, starting you off in the place where relational database modeling began. You have to begin at the beginning and start with the accepted formal approach, because an abstracted mathematical approach to building a model can be applied to any type of industry.

Normalization is an incremental or cumulative process in which each normal form layer adds to whatever normal forms have already been applied to a table. For example, 2nd normal form can only be applied to a table (or data model) that is already in 1st normal form, and similarly, 3rd normal form can only be applied to a table that is already in 2nd normal form. It follows that 3rd normal cannot be applied to a table in 4th normal form, because by definition a table in 4th normal form is cumulatively already in 3rd normal form, and so on.

> The demands of intensely busy applications and end-user needs can tend to necessitate relaxation of some of the rules of normalization sometimes in order to meet performance requirements—normal forms beyond 3rd normal form are often ignored as a result.

Each successive normal form is a refinement of the previous normal form, with normalization being an iterative or cumulative process, which is applied to each individual table until each table is at the desired level of uniqueness.

> Other terms used in relational database modeling to describe the desired level of uniqueness include *removal of duplication* and *reduction of redundancy*.

3.1.1 Defining the Normal Forms

The defined normal forms are the 1st, 2nd, and 3rd normal forms, in addition to the detailed Boyce-Codd, 4th, 5th, and Domain Key normal forms. Normal forms are the cumulative steps that are applied in the normalization process. For now, let's take a very brief look at the formal definitions of each normal form:

- **1st Normal Form (1NF).** Eliminate repeating elements or groups of elements within a table in which each row in the table relies on a primary key. This means that all rows in a table can be identified uniquely by a primary key, or that all columns other than the primary key must depend on the primary key—only then is a table in 1st normal form.

- **2nd Normal Form (2NF).** Provide for no partial dependencies on a concatenated key such that all non-key values must be fully functionally dependent on the primary key (non-key partial dependency exists when a column is fully dependent on a part of a composite primary key). This means that if there is a multi-column primary key, then none of the data in the columns must rely on only part of the columns in the key; each column must rely on all columns in the primary key—only then is a table in 2nd normal form.
- **3rd Normal Form (3NF).** There must be no dependencies on non-key columns that depend on keys (transitive dependencies must be eliminated). This means that a table is not in 3rd normal form if a column is indirectly determined by the primary key, because the column is functionally dependent on another column, where the other column is dependent on the primary key.
- **Beyond 3rd Normal Form.** These can be left for later on in this chapter, because they are rarely used in all but the most complex commercial applications.

It has been said that normalization describes the key, the whole key, and nothing but the key. What is not said is that one of the issues with normalization and normal forms is that there are multiple explanations for each normal form, all of which mean the same of course; but for the layman, reading a mathematically precise explanation can be confusing because any change in wording can change the meaning, even if using similar verbiage to describe the same concept in reverse.

3rd normal form is usually as far as even the most die-hard commercial relational database architect strives for, because for every additional level of normalization there are trade-offs, including additional complexity and the fact that for each additional layer of normalization, the joins (commands that read data from your database) get bigger, more complicated, and slower to return results. However, normalization also helps to prevent problems with data, and that can be very important in the precision of some applications where that is important.

In the next section you will read about my more intuitive approach to database design, bearing in mind that later on in this chapter you will get back to the accepted and more formal version of normalization. The objective is to enable your understanding and make you better able to cope with the addition of a more practical understanding as to why normalization and normal forms exist, and probably a better chance of making sense of normalization for yourself.

3.2 Intuitive Database Modeling

In a commercial environment, good performance can sometimes be more important than granular perfection in relational database design—and it is relatively common to have to manually fix data in a database if any imperfections arise as a result of not applying all the possible normal forms to data.

Normalization can be made a little easier to understand and to apply by offering a simplified interpretation of normalization just to get the novice started. In a perfect world, most relational database model designs are very similar, and as a result much of the basic database design for many applications is all more or less the same from a generic perspective in any industry, from accounting to manufacturing to retail to rocket science. There are often common factors across multiple industries, such as separation of repeated columns in master-detail relationships using a simplified version of 1st normal form, or also there is the pushing of static data into new tables using a simplified version of 2nd normal form. There are even some interesting simplified ways of applying 3rd normal form and beyond, such as uniquely identifying repetitions between many-to-many relationships.

Approaching data modeling from an intuitive perspective is for the most part easy and largely common sense, because it applies simple business knowledge to create a database model. There are of course numerous exceptional circumstances and special cases for which my intuitive interpretation of data modeling does not fill all needs 100%. However, in these situations, parts of the more refined and accepted approach of normalization and normal forms can be used; there's nothing stopping you using the accepted method (normalization and normal forms) in addition to some form of my intuitive approach to database modeling.

> My intuitive approach to data modeling is not actually normalization, but I sometimes use the term *normalization* so as to avoid readers misinterpreting and thinking I am no longer doing relational data modeling—and also because my intuitive approach is roughly based on normalization and normal forms.

3.2.1 Defining Data Modeling Intuitively

The following gives definition to a sequence of steps for relational data modeling, which is similar to normalization and normal forms, but it is also neither. What these steps do is to tell you as a data modeler to search for specific scenarios that can be obtained from application of normal forms, where these scenarios apply in most data models:

- **Master-Detail Relationship.** Remove repeating columns by creating a new table where the original table and the new table are linked together with a master-detail, one-to-many relationship (the original table is the master or parent table). Create primary keys on both tables where the detail table will have a composite primary key containing the master table primary key column as the prefix column of its primary key, and that prefix column is also a foreign key back to the master table.
- **Dynamic-Static Relationship.** Perform a seemingly similar function to that of creating a master-detail relationship as described for a master-detail relationship, but in this case create a new table where repeating *values* rather than repeating *columns* are moved to the new table. The result is a many-to-one relationship rather than a one-to-many relationship, created between the original table and the new table. The new table gets a primary key consisting of a single column, but this time the original table (the dynamic table) contains a foreign key pointing out to the primary key of the new table (the static table). Also, the foreign key is not part of the primary key in the original table.

It is important to note that master-detail and static-dynamic relationships can both be created using 1st normal form, 2nd normal form, and even 3rd normal form. This is partly because normal forms are cumulative, but also because from an intuitive perspective, the steps of normalization are more fluid and more generically applicable (an abstract approach) than my intuitive method of data modeling.

- **Many-to-Many Join Resolution Entity.** In this case two entities have a many-to-many relationship by replacing the many-to-many relationship with a new table. The new table then connects to the two original tables with two many-to-one relationships.

Remember that *entity* and *table* are synonymous.

- **Amalgamating Duplication from More than One Table.** If the same data is repeated in two static tables, then those shared columns can be moved to a new, shared table.
- **Splitting off a Transitive Dependency.** This is a case where a column is dependent on a second column in the same table, where only the first column is dependent on the primary key. The new table contains the first column as its primary key.
- **Removing a Calculated Value.** Calculated values that are dependent on other columns in the same table can be removed altogether because they can be recalculated. This is a special case of transitive dependence, because a calculated value is indirectly dependent on the primary key.
- **One-To-One NULL Table.** When a column in a table is often NULL, then that column can be moved to a new table, because it only depends on the primary key when it is not NULL.

The next step is to explain the various definitions described above using detailed examples.

3.2.2 *Master-Detail Relationship*

In this step, remove repeating columns by creating a new table, where the original table and the new table are linked together in a master-detail,

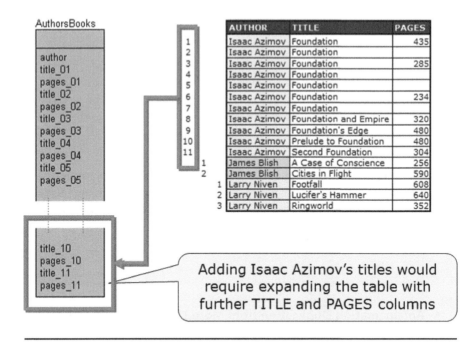

AuthorsBooks

author
title_01
pages_01
title_02
pages_02
title_03
pages_03
title_04
pages_04
title_05
pages_05

title_10
pages_10
title_11
pages_11

AUTHOR	TITLE	PAGES
Isaac Azimov	Foundation	435
Isaac Azimov	Foundation	
Isaac Azimov	Foundation	285
Isaac Azimov	Foundation	
Isaac Azimov	Foundation	
Isaac Azimov	Foundation	234
Isaac Azimov	Foundation	
Isaac Azimov	Foundation and Empire	320
Isaac Azimov	Foundation's Edge	480
Isaac Azimov	Prelude to Foundation	480
Isaac Azimov	Second Foundation	304
James Blish	A Case of Conscience	256
James Blish	Cities in Flight	590
Larry Niven	Footfall	608
Larry Niven	Lucifer's Hammer	640
Larry Niven	Ringworld	352

Adding Isaac Azimov's titles would require expanding the table with further TITLE and PAGES columns

Figure 3.1   A table that is not normalized or modeled at all.

one-to-many relationship. Figure 3.1 shows a table that is not normalized at all—and also exactly why creation of master-detail relationships is so essential. The reason is because the TITLE and PAGES columns are repeated, and you do not know how many times to repeat them—you do not want to keep having to change your table whenever an author writes a new book, you just want to change the data and not the data structure.

Figure 3.1 shows that splitting AUTHORSBOOKS into two tables will allow each author to have multiple books published. Not splitting the table includes repeated books and all authors in the same table as a repeating group in a single table. This is because each individual author requires repetitions for each book defined in each author row, and thus repetitions cannot be avoided for the table as shown on the left side of Figure 3.1 unless the table is split into two tables. In other words, supporting more than one book per author in the same row is inefficient and not scalable without frequent table structure changes. And so by splitting the table into two new tables, you provide the flexibility for authors to have one or a thousand books published, all using the same structure.

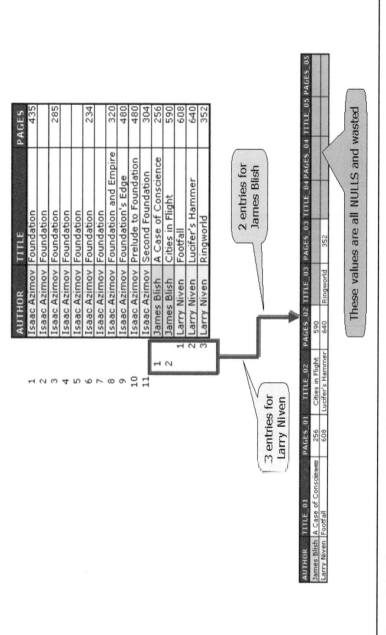

	AUTHOR	TITLE	PAGES
1	Isaac Azimov	Foundation	435
2	Isaac Azimov	Foundation	
3	Isaac Azimov	Foundation	285
4	Isaac Azimov	Foundation	
5	Isaac Azimov	Foundation	
6	Isaac Azimov	Foundation	234
7	Isaac Azimov	Foundation	
8	Isaac Azimov	Foundation and Empire	320
9	Isaac Azimov	Foundation's Edge	480
10	Isaac Azimov	Prelude to Foundation	480
11	Isaac Azimov	Second Foundation	304
	James Blish	A Case of Conscience	256
	James Blish	Cities in Flight	590
	Larry Niven	Footfall	608
	Larry Niven	Lucifer's Hammer	640
	Larry Niven	Ringworld	352

2 entries for James Blish

	1	2	3

3 entries for Larry Niven

AUTHOR	TITLE_01	PAGES_01	TITLE_02	PAGES_02	TITLE_03	PAGES_03	TITLE_04	PAGES_04	TITLE_05	PAGES_05
James Blish	A Case of Conscience	256	Cities in Flight	590						
Larry Niven	Footfall	608	Lucifer's Hammer	640	Ringworld	352				

These values are all NULLS and wasted

Figure 3.2 The AUTHORSBOOKS table with no break-down or normalization applied.

The lower part of the diagram shown in Figure 3.2 shows the detail of the AUTHORSBOOKS table shown in Figure 3.1, demonstrating that leaving a table with no break-down (or normalization) is neither sensible nor practical, because the result is an indefinable number of TITLE and PAGES columns.

In order to alleviate any potential confusion, Figure 3.3 shows how comma-delimited lists are used as another common method of displaying a table with no normalization; the comma-delimited list is a repeating group and is worse than repeating columns, because to break it down semantically, you have to parse the column every time you read it. The data shown in Figure 3.3 is identical to the data shown at the bottom of Figure 3.2, except with a slightly different and more usable structural representation—but it can still be improved upon.

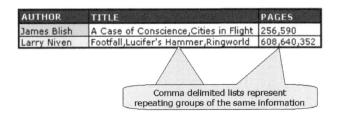

AUTHOR	TITLE	PAGES
James Blish	A Case of Conscience,Cities in Flight	256,590
Larry Niven	Footfall,Lucifer's Hammer,Ringworld	608,640,352

Comma delimited lists represent repeating groups of the same information

Figure 3.3 Using comma-delimited lists to represent a repeating group.

Figure 3.4 shows the application of a master-detail relationship to split the author and book information by removing repeating columns (repeating groups) and creating a new table, where the original table and the new table are linked in a master-detail or one-to-many relationship (one AUTHOR entry has many BOOK entries).

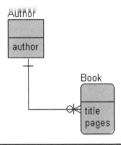

Figure 3.4 A master-detail relationship creates two tables for AUTHORSBOOKS.

Figure 3.5   Primary keys and the foreign key pointers between master and detail tables.

In Figure 3.5, primary keys are created on both tables, where the detail table will have a composite primary key of each author and each author's books. The composite primary key contains the master table primary key column as the prefix column of its primary key (the author's name), as well as its own primary key for titles written by each author. Also, the prefix column AUTHOR on the BOOK table is the foreign key pointing back to the master table's AUTHOR primary key, because the author's name determines which author wrote which books.

Figure 3.6 shows what the data looks like in the altered AUTHOR table and the new BOOK table, both of which were previously the single AUTHORSBOOKS table. Notice how the introduction of the relationship between the two tables allows any number of books for each author to be catered for, and so you do not have to create an undefined number of hard-coded columns in the form of an undefined number of TITLE and PAGES columns, as shown on the left side of Figure 3.1.

Looking at Figure 3.6, it is apparent that applying a master-detail relationship to the AUTHORSBOOKS table in Figure 3.1 has not actually saved any physical space; but as already stated, it has saved on unused metadata slots for numerous TITLE_*nn* and PAGES_*nn* columns. As a result, each column across a row contains different information, where titles and pages are not repeated a fixed number of times for each row—there is also no restriction on the number of books per author. The data is better organized in the master-detail, two-table format, and you also now have a relational database model. In addition, note that when you read the authors and books from the database, you can read AUTHOR.NAME and BOOK.NAME without having to refer to an unknown number of TITLE and PAGES columns, such as in

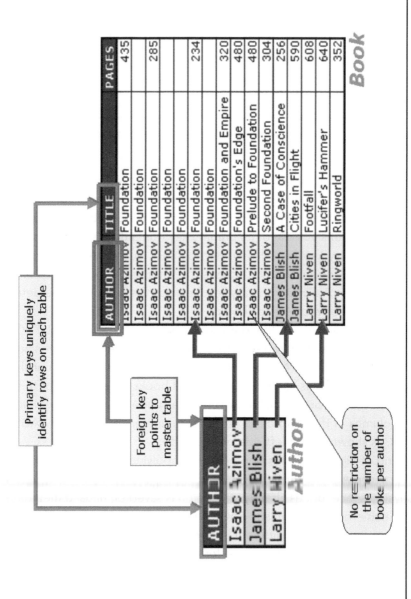

Figure 3.6 Authors and their books described by a master-detail relationship.

TITLE_01, PAGES_01 in hard-coded programs. So the functionality and thus the business logic is now embedded within the AUTHOR and BOOK tables in the database instead of in complicated programming code making hard-coded decisions about which TITLE and PAGES columns to read.

3.2.3 Dynamic-Static Relationship

Building dynamic-static relationships is similar in function to that of creating a master-detail relationship, except that this time a new table is created, where repeating groups of *values* rather than repeating groups of *columns* are moved to a new table. The result is a many-to-one relationship rather than a one-to-many relationship (one-to-many in the case of the master-detail relationship), now created between the original and the new tables. Of course, the many-to-one relationship and the one-to-many relationship are identical; however, the difference is the manner in which the relationship is arrived at, because dynamic and static data are being separated, as opposed to master and detail data being separated.

In Figure 3.7, the BOOK table has lookup information such as publisher and the subject of each book, where a publisher can publish many books, and many books fall under much fewer specific subjects. The BOOK table shown in Figure 3.7 had master-detail separation applied (remove repeated columns), in order to separate books from authors; now we should separate out publisher and subject information from books as well, but this time based on the fact that publishers and subjects describe books. So publishers print many books, and each subject contains many books. Also, publishers and subjects will be around for much longer than many books, and thus books are dynamic data, and in contrast publishers as well as subjects are more static in nature. Static data does not change very much compared to dynamic data—publishers and subjects do not change nearly as much as book data.

Figure 3.8 shows the initial stage of the separation of dynamic and static data, which removes static publisher and subject information from the more dynamic BOOK transaction table. The new table created in the dynamic-static relationship gets a primary key consisting of a single column in the static data table and a many-to-one relationship between dynamic and static data entities.

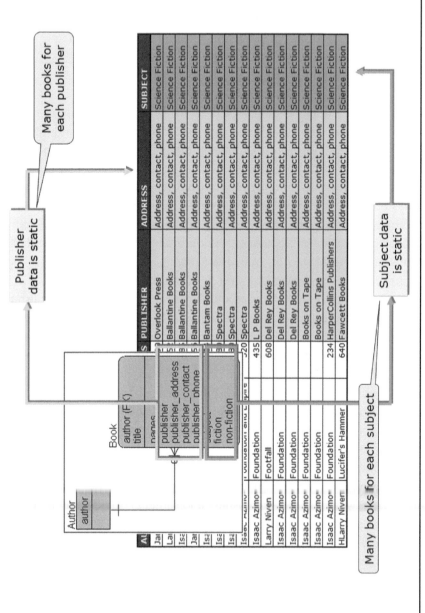

Figure 3.7 The BOOK table contains repeating values that can be separated out.

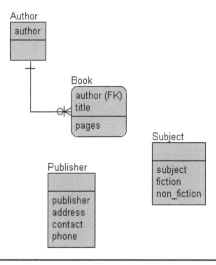

Figure 3.8   Separate information using the differences between dynamic and static data.

In Figure 3.9, many-to-one relationships are established between dynamic and static tables, creating many-to-one relationships of BOOK to PUBLISHER and BOOK to SUBJECT, where a publisher publishes multiple books and books are grouped into subjects.

In Figure 3.10, primary keys are created on both the PUBLISHER and SUBJECT tables in order to uniquely identify individual publishers and

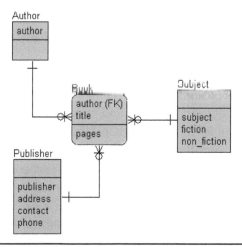

Figure 3.9   Create many-to-one relationships between dynamic and static tables.

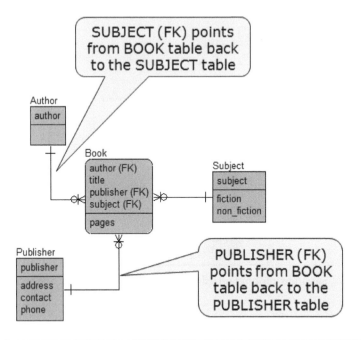

Figure 3.10   Primary keys in static tables are copied to the BOOK dynamic table as part of the dynamic table composite primary key.

subjects within their two respective tables. Identifying relationships as BOOK related to PUBLISHER, and BOOK related to SUBJECT causes the publisher and subject primary key values to be included in the composite primary key of the BOOK table, as shown in Figure 3.10 by the four-column composite primary key in the BOOK table.

You do not want the static table foreign keys to define unique rows in the BOOK table. So a correction is made in Figure 3.11 by changing the relationships between dynamic and static tables, from identifying to non-identifying (non-identifying relationships are shown in Figure 3.11 by dotted lines), removing the static foreign keys from the primary key. The existence of static data is not dependent on the existence of child dynamic data, and so a SUBJECT table entry is not dependent on the existence of any books within that subject. In other words, it is permissible to add the Science Fiction genre to the SUBJECT table without having to have any Science Fiction BOOK entries. Also, by changing the relationships from identifying to non-identifying, Figure 3.11 shows that primary keys for

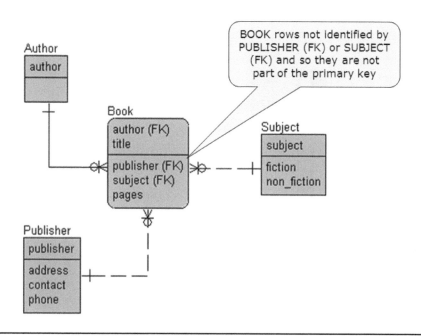

Figure 3.11   Non-identifying relationships prevent foreign primary keys from identifying objects uniquely.

publishers and subjects are no longer part of the composite primary key for the BOOK table.

It is important to understand that BOOK entries depend on the exis-tence of PUBLISHER and SUBJECT entries, and so publishers and sub-jects must exist for a book to exist—or every book must have a publisher and subject. On the contrary, the relationship between PUBLISHER and BOOK, or SUBJECT and BOOK, are in reality one-to-zero, one or many, which means that not all publishers absolutely have to have any titles published at any specific time, and also that there is not always a book available covering each available subject. This can also go further, in that BOOK.PUBLISHER (FK) and BOOK.SUBJECT (FK) columns can be defined as NULL, meaning that a BOOK row does not have to have a publisher or a subject.

Figure 3.12 shows what the data looks like in the altered BOOK table and the new PUBLISHER and SUBJECT tables. Multiple columns of publisher and subject information, which was previously duplicated on the BOOK table as shown in Figure 3.7, is now separated into the two new PUBLISHER

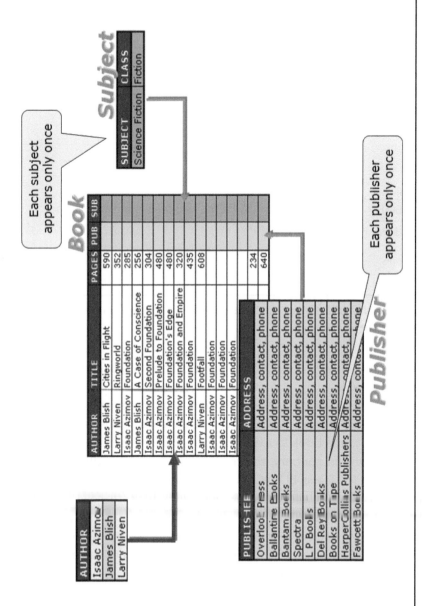

Figure 3.12 Books plus their respective publishers and subjects are better organized with dynamic-static many-to-one relationships.

and SUBJECT tables; duplicated publishers and subjects are also removed from the new tables, as their respective primary keys will not allow it. The data is gradually being divided up into more easily manageable pieces.

It is readily apparent from Figure 3.12 that organizing the BOOK table with more detailed dynamic-static relationships has saved on physical space. Also, duplication has been removed, in that there is only a single SUBJECT row for each subject, and that there are far fewer unique PUBLISHER rows. Data has become better organized by the separation of dynamic and static data into appropriate many-to-one relationships.

> A dynamic-static relationship creates a static data table that is also known as a lookup, domain, or lookup table.

3.2.4 Advanced Relationships

There are many different ways to break down tables beyond the basic master-detail and dynamic-static table relationships, and some of those are covered in this section on advanced relationships.

3.2.4.1 Many-to-Many Join Resolution Entity

Figure 3.13 shows a many-to-many relationship in which an employee can be assigned many tasks and a task can be assigned to many employees. A many-to-many join resolution entity can be created to allow for a unique employee task assignment to be accessed.

Figure 3.14 shows employees and tasks prior to the addition of the many-to-many join resolution entity, the transformation of which is shown in Figure 3.13 with the addition of the new ASSIGNMENT table. Without the ASSIGNMENT table, searching for the employee Columbia would return three tasks. Similarly, if searching for the third task as shown in Figure 3.14, two employees would always be returned; there are no unique employee assignments without the ASSIGNMENT table. A problem would arise with this situation when searching for an attribute specific to a particular assignment where an assignment is a single task assigned to a single employee, such as how long the employee took to complete a particular task (the hours employees spent working on an assignment). Without the

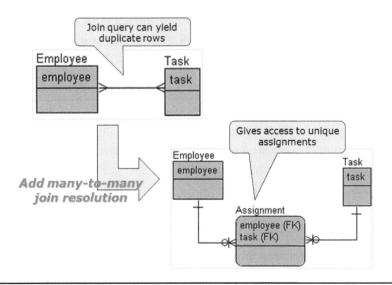

Figure 3.13   Resolving a many-to-many relationship into a new table.

new ASSIGMENT table created by the many-to-many join resolution entity of the ASSIGNMENT table as shown in Figure 3.13, finding a unique assignment would be impossible.

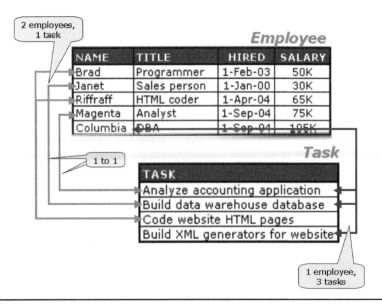

Figure 3.14   A many-to-many relationship finds duplicate rows when unique rows are sought.

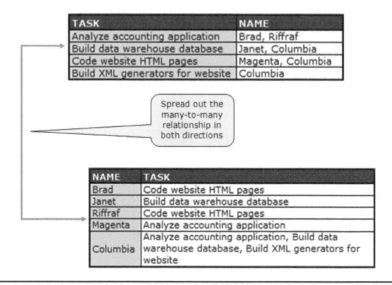

TASK	NAME
Analyze accounting application	Brad, Riffraf
Build data warehouse database	Janet, Columbia
Code website HTML pages	Magenta, Columbia
Build XML generators for website	Columbia

Spread out the many-to-many relationship in both directions

NAME	TASK
Brad	Code website HTML pages
Janet	Build data warehouse database
Riffraf	Code website HTML pages
Magenta	Analyze accounting application
Columbia	Analyze accounting application, Build data warehouse database, Build XML generators for website

Figure 3.15   Spreading out the values in a many-to-many relationship.

Both sides of the many-to-many relationship shown in Figure 3.14 have been spread out in Figure 3.15 just to put the data into a clearer perspective.

3.2.4.2 Amalgamating Duplication from More than One Table

What you want to do here is to extract common columns across multiple tables and place them into a new table that is shared by the original tables. This type of situation is common to static data tables where multiple static tables have the same type descriptions such as that shown in Figure 3.16. In Figure 3.16 columns common to both the CUSTOMER and SUPPLIER tables can be moved from both CUSTOMER and SUPPLIER tables, into a new table as shown by the creation of the FOREIGN_EXCHANGE table in Figure 3.15.

There are two reasons for allowing the removal of common information from the CUSTOMER and SUPPLIER tables in this situation:

Currency coding and rate information does not depend on CUSTOMER and SUPPLIER primary keys, even though which currency they use does depend on who the customer or supplier is, based on which country they do business in.

The CURRENCY and EXCHANGE_RATE columns in the pre-transformation tables are transitively dependant on CUSTOMER and SUPPLIER primary

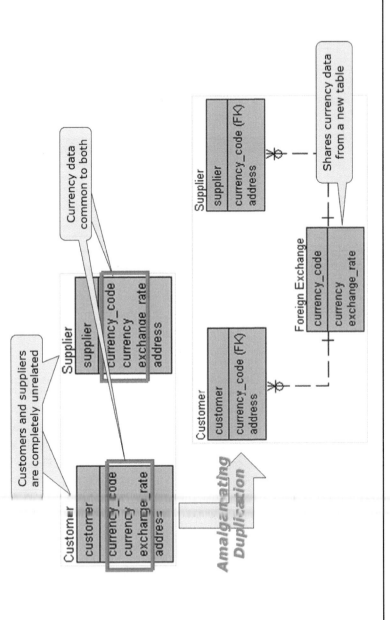

Figure 3.16 Amalgamating duplication from more than one table.

keys because they depend on the CURRENCY_CODE, which in turn does depend on CUSTOMER and SUPPLIER primary keys.

The transformation shown in Figure 3.16 will decrease the size of the database in general, because repeated copies of CURRENCY and EXCHANGE_RATE columns have been reduced into the FOREIGN_EXCHANGE table (completely removed from the CUSTOMER and SUPPLIER tables). However, there is also one very good reason that this type of granularization of data can be risky, because queries reading customers or suppliers will have to read and join two static tables rather than just read the CUSTOMER or SUPPLIER tables—bigger joins can make for inefficient applications.

> In the previous section, I have deliberately contradicted myself, saying first one thing and then the opposite. This approach is not intended to confuse but only to show you that data modeling is by no means an exact science. In this specific case, creating multiple layers in static data tables can be elegant during development but can cause serious performance problems perhaps even years later in production. What works to begin with does not always work out well in the long run, and this is one thing you can look for when trying to make an application and database perform faster.

3.2.4.3 Splitting Off a Transitive Dependency

A transitive dependency occurs where one column depends on another, which in turn depends on a third column, the third column typically being the primary key. A state of transitive dependency can also be interpreted as a column not being entirely dependent on the primary key. Figure 3.17 shows a very clear transitive dependency from CITY to DEPARTMENT and the EMPLOYEE primary key column.

In Figure 3.17, a transitive dependency exists because it is assumed that each employee is assigned to a particular department and that each department within a company is exclusively based in one specific city. Therefore the city depends indirectly (transitively) on an employee, and so the DEPARTMENT table can be separated out. Again, this type of normalization might generate too many tables and compromise overall join efficiency.

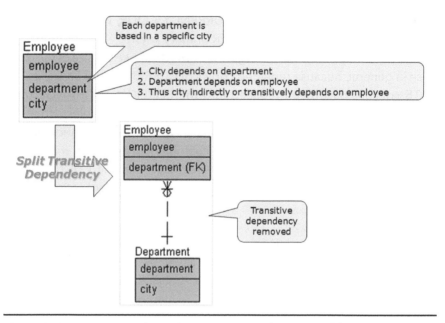

Figure 3.17   A transitive dependency separation from one table to a new table.

3.2.4.4 Splitting Off a Calculated Value

Figure 3.18 shows a calculated value being stored in a table, where that calculated value is derived from values in other columns that are in the same table. This calculated column is not fully dependent on the primary key (but is transitively dependent on the primary key), and thus does not necessarily require a new table—therefore calculated columns can be removed.

Calculated values are usually added for the sake of efficiency in order to avoid constant recalculation, so retaining them and even adding new calculated columns is often better for general database efficiency. Data warehouses often store pre-calculated values for the purpose of efficient queries and reporting.

3.2.4.5 One-to-One NULL Table

Figure 3.19 shows removal of two columns from a table called EDITION that will often have NULL values, creating the new table called RANK. The result is a zero or one-to-one relationship between the RANK and

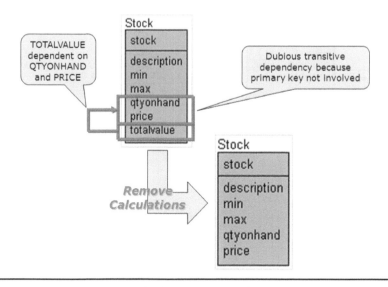

Figure 3.18   Remove transitively dependent calculated columns.

EDITION tables, meaning that if a RANK row exists, then a corresponding EDITION row must exist as well. In the opposite case, an EDITION
row can exist and a RANK row does not have to exist for each edition.
This opposite case accounts for an edition of a publication having no
RANK and INGRAM_UNITS values—a very recently published publication might not have any statistical information such as rankings and
Ingram numbers.

Figure 3.20 shows a data picture of the granularized structure shown
at the bottom right of the diagram in Figure 3.19, where the often NULL
valued RANK and INGRAM_UNITS columns are moved into a new table,
creating a one-to-one or zero relationship and removing a lot of NULL values from the EDITION table.

In the case of the tables shown in the model from Figure 3.19 and sample table data from Figure 3.20, the RANK and INGRAM_UNITS columns
are not co-dependent; they do not depend on each other and are completely unrelated. It is quite possible that one column may be NULL valued
and the other not. Therefore, in the extreme, the data model could include
two new tables, as shown in Figure 3.21, with a new table for the RANK column and another new table for the INGRAM_UNITS column, but this is too
much granularity in my opinion. Disk space is cheap compared with CPU

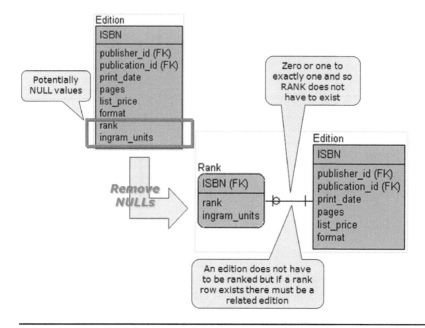

Figure 3.19   Removing NULL columns to new tables.

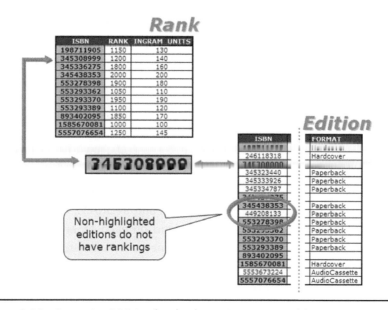

Figure 3.20   Removing NULL valued columns into a new table.

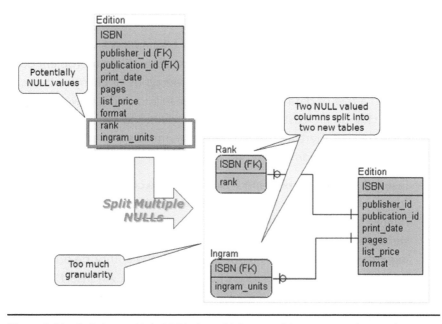

Figure 3.21   Splitting multiple NULLs in multiple new tables is too much granularization.

and RAM, and what you can save on space you will lose in performance with more tables leading to bigger SQL joins.

This level of granularity, separating NULL valued columns into separate tables is going much too far, making too many little-bitty pieces and introducing too many tables into queries, and I do not recommend this level of detail; it is also largely unnecessary in the larger modern databases because NULL values do not occupy any extra space.

3.3 Data Model Design with Normalization

Normalization using normal forms is the accepted method of data model design for relational databases. In general normalization removes duplication, minimizes redundant chunks of data, makes things better organized, and uses physical space more efficiently. Before going into demonstrating the precise definitions of normal forms, some specifics need to be explained briefly to help you better understand the reasoning behind normalization and some of its normal forms.

3.3.1 Anomalies

Relational database theory is interested in eliminating situations from a database that contradict the integrity of that data. When a problem does occur, it is called an *anomaly*. There are three types of changes that can be made to a row of data in a table: (1) an insert to add a new row, (2) an update to change an existing row, and (3) a delete to remove an existing row. It follows that there are three types of anomalies in the form of insert, update, and delete anomalies:

- **Insert Anomaly.** A row cannot be added to a child table (contains the foreign key that links to a parent table containing the foreign key's related primary key), unless the row exists in the parent table, and the same parent cannot be added more than once. In other words, adding a new book in Figure 3.5 requires that the author be added first and also that the author does not already exist. An insert anomaly occurs when one of these rules is broken.

- **Delete Anomaly.** A row cannot be deleted from a parent table unless all related child rows are deleted first. An exception is a cascade deletion when deletion of a parent row automatically deletes all child rows in all child-related tables, before deleting the row in the parent table. For instance, using Figure 3.5 again, deleting an author requires initial deletion of any books that an author might already have published. If an author can be deleted and books are left in the database without corresponding parent authors, then the BOOK table rows would become known as *orphaned rows*, and the books would be logically inaccessible. Of course in the case of a cascade deletion, all books for an author are automatically deleted before a specific author is deleted. A delete anomaly occurs when a parent row is deleted without related child rows being deleted first.

- **Update Anomaly.** This situation is similar to deletion, in that in cascading it needs to be ensured that any primary key updates are propagated to related child table foreign keys; the change can also be prohibited by not allowing cascading. Another form of this anomaly is ensuring that if multiple rows are updated at once, all multiple rows are actually required to be updated. So an update anomaly happens when a change occurs in a parent primary key that is not propagated to related child table foreign key rows, or a change occurs in a child table that is not propagated to a related table's parent table primary key.

3.3.2 Dependency and Determinants

Dependency implies that something depends on something else, and a determinant is the reverse or inverse of dependency, which implies that something determines something else; the details are as follows:

- **Functional Dependency.** Y is functionally dependent on X if the value of Y is determined by X. In other words, if Y = X + 1, then the value of X will determine the resultant value of Y. Thus Y is dependent on X as a function of the value of X. Figure 3.22 demonstrates functional dependency by showing that the currency being Pounds depends on the FXCODE value being GBP.

FXCODE	CURRENCY	RATE	
ALL	Leke		
BGN	Leva		Bulgaria
CYP	Pounds		Cyprus
CZK	Koruny		Czech Republic
DKK	Kroner	5.8157	Denmark
DM	Deutsche Marks	1.5	Germany
HUF	Forint		Hungary
ISK	Kronur		Iceland
MTL	Liri		Malta
NOK	Krone	6.5412	Norway
PLN	Zlotych		Poland
ROL	Lei		
SEK	Kronor	7.087	Sweden
CHF	Francs	1.217	Switzerland
GBP	Pounds	0.5385155	United Kingdom

> DM determines that the currency is Deutsche Marks

> Pounds is dependent on the code being GBP

Figure 3.22   Functional dependency and the determinant.

- **Determinant.** The determinant in the description of functional dependency and in the previous point is X, because X determines the value Y, at least partially, because 1 is added to X as well. In Figure 3.22, the determinant of the currency being Deutsche Marks is that the value of FXCODE be DM. The determinant is thus FXCODE.

> A determinant is the inversion, the opposite or
> the reverse of functional dependency.

Transitive Dependence. Z is transitively dependent on X when X determines Y and Y determines Z. Transitive dependence thus describes that Z is indirectly dependent on X through its relationship with Y. In Figure 3.22

the foreign exchange rates in the RATE column contains ratios against the US Dollar and thus all are dependent on CURRENCY. The currency in turn is dependent on COUNTRY. Thus the rate is dependent on the currency, which is in turn dependent on the country. Therefore RATE is transitively dependent on COUNTRY.

Candidate Key. A candidate key, a potential key, a possible key, or a permissible key is a column or combination of columns that can act as a primary key column for a table, and that primary key uniquely identifies each row in the table. Figure 3.23 shows five different variations of one table, all of whom have valid primary keys, some with one column and some with more than one column. The number of options displayed in Figure 3.23 is a little ridiculous but demonstrates the concept.

- **Full Functional Dependence.** This situation occurs where X determines Y but X combined with Z do not determine Y, as only X determines Y,

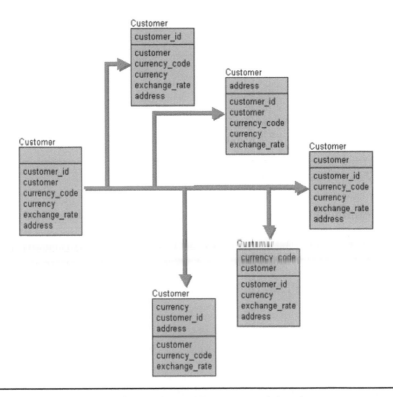

Figure 3.23   A table with five and possibly more candidate keys.

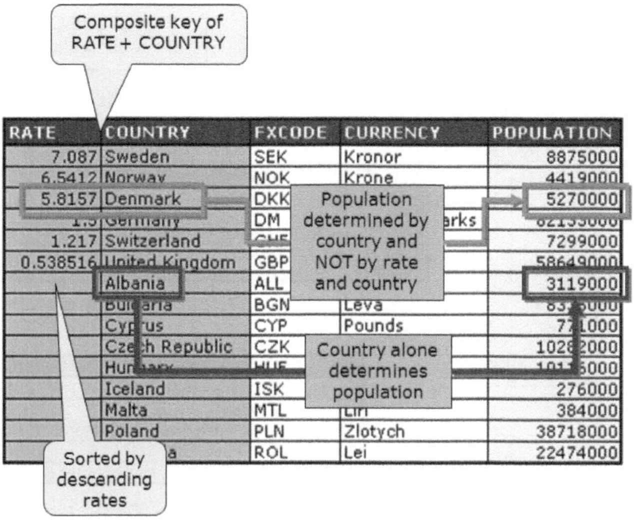

Composite key of RATE + COUNTRY

RATE	COUNTRY	FXCODE	CURRENCY	POPULATION
7.087	Sweden	SEK	Kronor	8875000
6.5412	Norway	NOK	Krone	4419000
5.8157	Denmark	DKK	Population	5270000
1.9	Germany	DM	determined by arks	82135000
1.217	Switzerland	CHE	country and	7299000
0.538516	United Kingdom	GBP	NOT by rate	58649000
	Albania	ALL	and country	3119000
	Bulgaria	BGN	Leva	83?000
	Cyprus	CYP	Pounds	771000
	Czech Republic	CZK	Country alone	1028000
	Hungary	HUF	determines	1015000
	Iceland	ISK	population	276000
	Malta	MTL	Liri	384000
	Poland	PLN	Zlotych	38718000
		ROL	Lei	22474000

Sorted by descending rates

Figure 3.24 Full functional dependence.

and Z has no effect on Y. In other words, Y depends on X and X alone. If Y depends on X with anything else, then there is not full functional dependence between X and Y. Figure 3.24 shows that POPULATION is dependent on COUNTRY but not on the combination of RATE (currency exchange rate) and COUNTRY. Therefore, there is a full functional dependency between POPULATION and COUNTRY, because RATE is irrelevant to POPULATION.

- **Multiple Valued Dependency.** A commonly used example of a multi-valued dependency is a column containing a comma-delimited list or collection of some kind. A collection could be an array of values of the same type, where those multiple values are dependent as a whole on the primary key. More precisely:
  - o A trivial multi-valued dependency occurs between two columns when they are the only two columns in the table, where one is the primary key and the other the multi-valued list. A trivial multi-valued dependency is shown at the bottom right of the diagram in Figure 3.25, in the list of skills.
  - o A non-trivial multi-valued dependency occurs when there are other columns in the table, as shown at the top right of the diagram

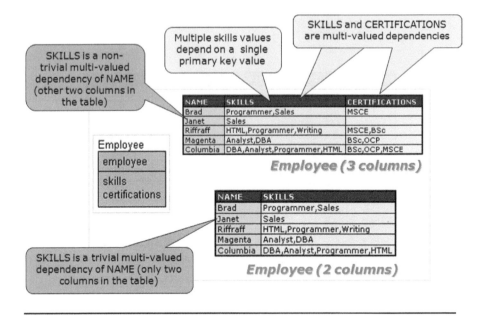

Figure 3.25   Multiple valued dependencies.

shown in Figure 3.25, in the list of skills and certifications. It is also important to note that skills and certifications are both dependant on the name of the person, but they are not dependant on each other.

- **Cyclic Dependency.** The dictionary definition of the word *cyclic* is a circular pattern, recurrent, closed ring, or a circular chain structure. In the context of the relational database model, cyclic dependence means that X is dependent on Y, and Y is also dependent on X, directly or indirectly. Cyclic dependence therefore indicates a logically circular pattern of interdependence. Cyclic dependence typically occurs with tables containing a composite primary key with three or more columns, where, for instance, three columns are related in pairs to one another. In other words, X relates to Y, Y relates to Z, and X relates to Z.

That covers some of the necessary jargon; now let's briefly revisit the definitions of normal forms before you get to see examples.

3.3.3 Defining Normal Forms Again

Before going through each of the normal forms in detail and by example, let's begin by reiterating the definitions of normal forms but this time covering all the normal forms explicitly:

- **1st Normal Form (1NF).** Eliminate repeating elements or groups of elements within a table where each row in the table relies on a primary key. This means that all rows in a table can be identified uniquely by a primary key, or that all columns other than the primary key must depend on the primary key. Only then is a table in 1st normal form.
- **2nd Normal Form (2NF).** Provide for no partial dependencies on a concatenated key where all non-key values must be fully functionally dependent on the primary key, such that no partial dependencies are allowed, and a partial dependency exists when a column is fully dependant on a part of a composite primary key. This means that if there is a multi-column primary key, then none of the data in the columns must rely on only part of the columns in the key—each column must rely on all columns in the primary key. Only then is a table in 2nd normal form.
- **3rd Normal Form (3NF).** There must be no dependencies on non-key attributes such that transitive dependencies must be eliminated. This means that a table is not in 3rd normal form if a column is indirectly determined by the primary key, because the column is functionally dependent on another column, where the other column is dependent on the primary key.
- **BCNF or Boyce-Codd Normal Form.** Every determinant in a table is a candidate key, but if there is only one candidate key, then 3rd normal form and Boyce-Codd normal form are the same thing.
- **4th Normal Form.** Eliminate multiple sets of multi-valued dependencies.
- **5th Normal Form.** Eliminate cyclic dependencies. 5th normal form is also known as *Projection normal form* or *PJNF*.
- **DKNF or Domain Key Normal Form.** DKNF is the ultimate application of normalization and is more a measurement of conceptual state, as opposed to a transformation process in itself.

> Again, normalization describes the key,
> the whole key, and nothing but the key.

3.3.4 1st Normal Form

1st normal form has the following characteristics:

- Eliminates repeating groups.
- Defines primary keys.
- All rows must be identified uniquely with a primary key, where a primary key is a type of key that cannot contain duplicate values.
- All columns other than the primary key must depend on the primary key, either directly or indirectly.
- All columns must contain a single value (no comma-delimited lists).
- All values in each column must be of the same datatype.
- Requires creation of a new table to move the repeating groups out of the original table.

> By definition, applying 1st normal form is a requirement for a database to be relational.

Figure 3.26 shows a table that is not normalized at all and you can apply 1st normal form to it:

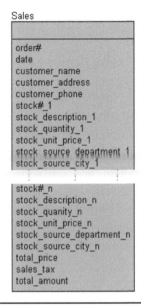

Figure 3.26   A table with no normalization.

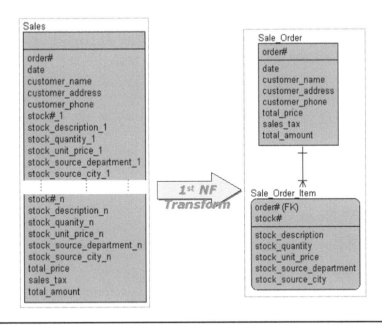

Figure 3.27   1st normal form transformation of the SALES table in Figure 3.26.

1. Put the SALES table shown in Figure 3.26 into 1st normal form.
2. Create a new table with the appropriate columns.
3. Remove the appropriate columns from the original table.
4. Create primary keys in the original and new tables.
5. Create the one-to-many relationship between the original and new tables by defining the foreign key in the new table.

Figure 3.27 shows the result of application of 1st normal form, which requires the removal of repeating groups into a new table.

1. The SALES table contains orders with lines on each order represented by each stock item on the order.
2. Figure 3.27 shows the desired 1st normal form transformation.

Figure 3.27 shows repeated sales order item entries in the form of stock item entries moved to the SALE_ORDER_ITEM table, linking back to the renamed SALE_ORDER table (the SALE_ORDER table is renamed from the original SALES table). The two tables are linked by a one-to-many relationship between the SALE_ORDER and SALE_ORDER_ITEM tables using the primary key called ORDER# on the SALE_ORDER table, which is duplicated to the SALE_ORDER_ITEM table as the ORDER# (FK) column, part of the SALE_ORDER_ITEM table composite primary key.

> In the particular case of Figure 3.27, the relationship is in reality a one-to-one or many relationship excluding zeros. In other words, you cannot have a sale without at least one item sold—you have to sell something in the sales order item table in order to create a sales order.

3.3.5 2nd Normal Form

2nd normal form has the following characteristics:

- The table must already be in 1st normal form.
- All non-key values must be fully functionally dependent on the primary key. In other words, non-key columns that are not completely and individually dependent on the primary key are not allowed.
- Partial dependencies must be removed. A partial dependency is a special type of functional dependency which exists when a column is fully dependent on a part of the composite primary key.
- Remove columns that are independent of the primary key (this states the above two points in a different way).
- Requires creation of a new table to separate the partially dependent part of the primary key and its dependent columns.

Figure 3.28 shows two tables in 1st normal form that you can use to apply 2nd normal form to:

1. Put the SALE_ORDER and SALE_ORDER_ITEM tables shown in Figure 3.28 into 2nd normal form.
2. Create two new tables with the appropriate columns.
3. Remove the appropriate columns from the original tables.
4. Create primary keys in the new tables.
5. Create the many-to-one relationships between the original tables and the new tables, defining and placing foreign keys appropriately.

And so 2nd normal form requires removal to new tables of columns that are partially dependent on primary keys.

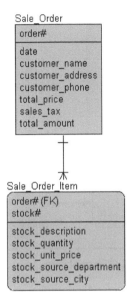

Figure 3.28 Two tables in 1st normal form.

1. Create the CUSTOMER table to remove static data from the SALE_ORDER table.
2. Create the STOCK_ITEM table to remove static data from the SALE_ORDER_ITEM table.
3. Figure 3.29 shows all four tables after the 2nd normal form transformation.

Figure 3.29 shows creation of two new tables where both new tables establish many-to-one relationships between the original table and the new table (1st normal form built one-to-many relationships between original and new tables). Another difference is that the foreign key columns appear in the original tables rather than the new tables as a result of the direction of the relationship between the original table and the new table.

> There is a one-to-many or zero relationship between customers and sales in Figure 3.29, which means that someone can be a customer even when they have not as yet bought anything.

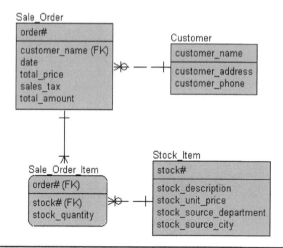

Figure 3.29   Four tables in 2nd normal form.

3.3.6 3rd Normal Form

3rd normal form has the following characteristics:

- The table must be in 2nd normal form.
- Eliminate transitive dependencies. A transitive dependency is where a column is indirectly determined by the primary key because that column is functionally dependent on a second column, where that second column is dependent on the primary key.
- Or said another way, every column in a table that is not a key field must be directly dependent on the primary key, and if it is not it should probably be in another subset or related table.

> Remember that field and column are synonymous.

- Create a new table to contain any separated columns.

And now you can try applying 3rd normal form where Figure 3.30 shows four tables:

1. Assume that any particular department within the company is located in only one city. Thus assume that a city is always dependent upon which department a sales order occurred within.

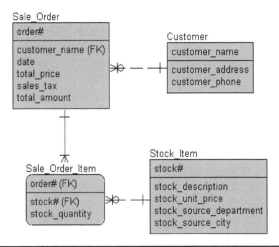

Figure 3.30 Four tables in 2nd normal form.

2. Put the SALE_ORDER and STOCK_ITEM tables into 3rd normal form.
3. Remove some calculated columns and create a new table.
4. Remove the appropriate columns from the original table to a new table.
5. Create a primary key in the new table.
6. Create a many-to-one relationship between the original table and the new table, defining and placing a foreign key appropriately.

The solution of applying 3rd normal form elimination of transitive dependencies is required:

1. Create the STOCK_SOURCE_DEPARTMENT table as the city is dependent upon the department, which is in turn dependant on the primary key; this eliminates a transitive dependency.
2. Remove the TOTAL_PRICE, SALES_TAX, and TOTAL_AMOUNT columns from the SALE_ORDER table, as these columns are all transitively dependent on the sum of STOCK_QUANTITY and STOCK_UNIT_PRICE values, both of which are now in two other tables.
3. Figure 3.31 shows the desired 3rd normal form transformations.

Figure 3.31 shows creation of one new table and the removal of three dependent columns from the SALE_ORDER table. The new table has its primary key placed into the STOCK_ITEM table as a foreign key.

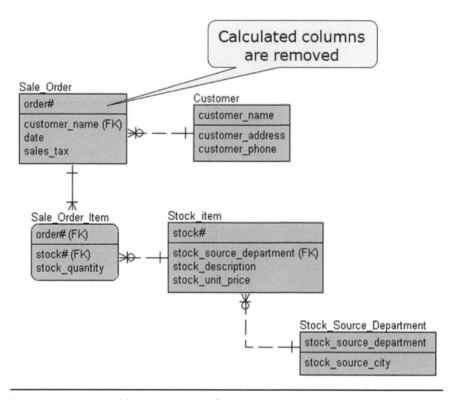

Figure 3.31   Five tables in 3rd normal form.

3.3.7 Advanced Normalization Beyond 3rd Normal Form

Beyond 3rd normal form are Boyce-Codd normal form (BCNF), 4th normal form, 5th normal form, and Domain Key normal form (DKNF)—that might be just one or two normal forms too many to deal with from the layman's perspective. It always seems so inconceivable that relational database models can become so horribly complicated, because often the essentials are by and large covered by 1st, 2nd, and almost always 3rd normal form transformations.

Some of the biggest problems with going beyond 3rd normal form are complexity and performance issues, because too much granularity can introduce complexity in a relational database. After all, a relational structure is not an object structure, and object structures become more simplistic as they are further reduced—in some respects, over-granularization of a relational model can make that relational model much more complex than it needs to be from the perspective of programming and application performance. As already stated more than once, in a relational database, the more normalization that is applied, then the greater the number of tables created; the greater the number of tables in a relational data model, then the larger SQL query joins become, and the larger joins become the poorer database performance. Extremes in normalization rarely apply in fast-paced commercial environments, because commercial operations require that a job is done efficiently and cost effectively.

3.3.7.1 Boyce-Codd Normal Form

BC normal form has the following characteristics:

- A table must be in 3rd normal form.
- A table can have only one candidate key.

> A candidate key is any key that has potential for being a table's primary key. A table is not allowed more than one primary key, because referential integrity requires it. It would be impossible to check foreign keys against more than one primary key, and thus referential integrity would be automatically invalid and unenforceable.

BCNF or Boyce-Codd normal form is an odd one, as it is a little like a special case of 3rd normal form. BCNF requires that every determinant in a table is a candidate key. If there is only one candidate key, then a table is already in both 3rd normal form and Boyce-Codd normal form. What does this mean? Firstly, what is a determinant again? A determinant is a column whose value other columns may depend on for their values. What is a candidate key? Some tables can be uniquely identified by more than one column or combination of columns. Each one of these is a potential primary key that can uniquely identify rows in a table, and thus they are candidate keys, or at least potential primary keys.

The left side of the diagram in Figure 3.32 shows an example of a table with both a surrogate key and a natural key. Surrogate keys are added to tables to replace natural keys, because surrogate keys are more efficient and easier to manage than natural keys; also there needs to be a unique qualifier on a table in order to make sure that it is not duplicated. Two

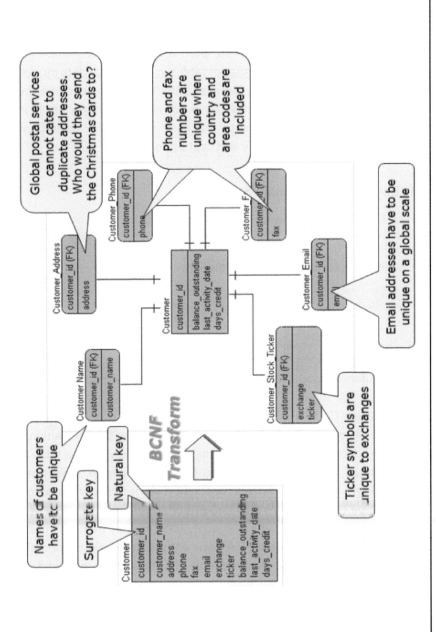

Figure 3.32 Using Boyce-Codd normal form to separate all candidate keys into separate tables.

customers with the same name could cause a problem when it comes to sending them both an invoice at the end of the month, so it is prudent to use a surrogate key as the primary key. The right side of the diagram in Figure 3.32 shows a BCNF breakdown into multiple tables created from the original table, for any values that are potentially unique. This is what the purest form of BCNF essentially requires, which to me is taking normalization into too much detail for practicality.

Unique key tables created on the right side of the diagram in Figure 3.32 show all the conceivable possibilities of separating tables into individual units, accessible by the single primary key column CUSTOMER_ID because the separated columns are unique.

> Dividing tables up like that shown in Figure 3.32 can result in some serious inefficiencies, because too many tables will require large and potentially inefficient SQL join queries.

Boyce-Codd normal form specifies that a candidate key is by definition a unique key, and thus a potential primary key. If a table contains more than one candidate key (primary key), then there may be cause for anomalies. BCNF divides a table up into multiple tables in order to ensure that no single table has more than one potential primary key, which is potentially too much detail for commercial OLTP environments.

3.3.7.2   4th Normal Form

4th normal form has the following characteristics:

- A table must be in 3rd normal form or BCNF with 3rd normal form.
- Multi-valued dependencies must be transformed into functional dependencies. This implies that one value and not multiple values are dependent on a single primary key value.
- Eliminate multiple sets of multiple valued or multi-valued dependencies, sometimes described as non-trivial multi-valued dependencies.

A multiple valued set is a column containing a comma-delimited list or collection of some kind, which can be resolved by 1st normal form. However, 4th normal form deals with a table that has multiple dependent lists, where those dependent lists are unrelated to each other.

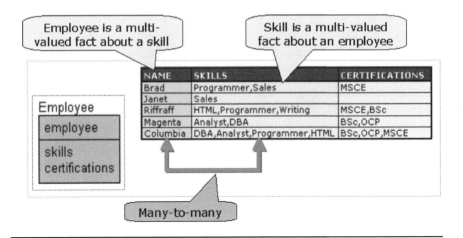

Figure 3.33   Multi-valued lists not in 4th normal form.

Figure 3.33 shows employees with variable numbers of both skills and certifications, where those skills and certifications are unrelated to each other and stored as comma-delimited list arrays in single columns in the EMPLOYEE table.

And so in Figure 3.34 you can see that there are two many to many relationships between the employee and the employees related skills and certifications, but that there is no relationship between the skills and certifications specifically.

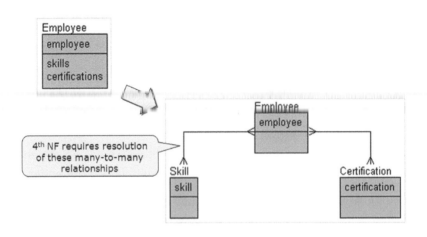

Figure 3.34   Multiple multi-valued dependencies equates to multiple many-to-many.

Figure 3.35 shows all the possible combinations for one employee only, showing all possible skill and certification possibilities, including nulls for both skill and certification. The result is a data set showing a single table that is denormalized because of all the repetitions (all possible combinations). In reality, every employee can be related to every skill and to every certification, including neither and none represented by null values. Representing the actual relationships requires only inclusion of a lot of duplication.

NAME	SKILLS	CERTIFICATIONS
Brad	Programmer	MSCE
Brad	Programmer	BSc
Brad	Programmer	OCP
Brad	Programmer	
Brad	Sales	MSCE
Brad	Sales	BSc
Brad	Sales	OCP
Brad	Sales	
Brad	HTML	MSCE
Brad	HTML	BSc
Brad	HTML	OCP
Brad	HTML	
Brad	Writing	MSCE
Brad	Writing	BSc
Brad	Writing	OCP
Brad	Writing	
Brad	Analyst	MSCE
Brad	Analyst	BSc
Brad	Analyst	OCP
Brad	Analyst	
Brad	DBA	MSCE
Brad	DBA	BSc
Brad	DBA	OCP
Brad	DBA	

Figure 3.35   Multiple unrelated multi-valued dependencies can produce a lot of duplication

The problem with the solution as shown in Figure 3.35 is that you do not ensure against update anomalies because there is nothing stopping a programmer from making an error and putting a skill into a certification, and so on and so forth. In short, it is better to divide the non-dependent data into two separate tables in which duplication is removed. And so Figure 3.36 resolves the many-to-many relationships into EMPLOYEE_SKILL and EMPLOYEE_CERTIFICATION tables, shown as many-to-many relationships in Figure 3.34. The many-to-many relationships resolved into one-to-many relationships in Figure 3.36 contain composites of employee names, original skills, and certifications arrays, with arrays spread into separate rows.

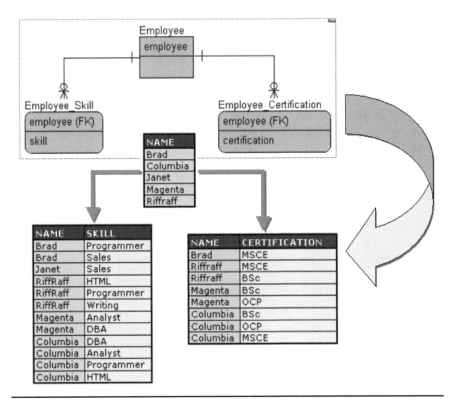

Figure 3.36   Data for the classic example 4th normal form as shown in Figure 3.35.

Essentially 4th normal form attempts to generate sets or arrays spread into separate rows in separate tables, making each individual row perhaps easier to access when doing exact match searching.

3.3.7.3 5th Normal Form

5th normal form has the following characteristics:

- A table must be in 4th normal form.
- Cyclic dependencies must be eliminated. A cyclic dependency is simply something which depends on one thing, where that one thing is either directly or indirectly dependent on itself.

5th normal form is also known as *projection normal form* or *PJNF*. The term *projection* is used to describe new tables containing subsets of data

from the original table. A cyclic dependency is a form of circular dependency where three pairs result as a combination of a single three-column
composite primary key table—those three pairs being column 1 with column 2, column 2 with column 3, and column 1 with column 3. In other
words, the cyclic dependency is that everything is related to everything
else, including itself, and so there is a permutation excluding repetitions
that are invalid because they can cause update anomaly errors. If tables
are joined again using a three-table join, then the resulting rows will be the
same as that present in the original table. It is a stated requirement of the
validity of 5th normal form that the post-transformation join must match
rows for a query on the pre-transformation table.

   5th normal form can be demonstrated as follows. We begin by creating a
three-column composite primary key table, and here is your very first introduction in this book to the types of commands that are used in relational
databases to create objects such as tables and keys:

```
CREATE TABLE Employees
(
        project VARCHAR2(32) NOT NULL,
        employee VARCHAR2(32) NOT NULL,
        manager VARCHAR2(32) NOT NULL,
        PRIMARY KEY (project,employee,manager)
);
```

   Note the composite primary key on all three columns present in the
table. Now add some rows to the table, as shown also in the graphic in
Figure 3.37:

```
INSERT INTO Employees VALUES('Analysis','Brad','Joe');
INSERT INTO Employees VALUES('Analysis','Riffraff','Jim');
INSERT INTO Employees VALUES('Analysis','Magenta','Jim');
INSERT INTO Employees VALUES('DW','Janet','Larry');
INSERT INTO Employees VALUES('DW','Brad','Larry');
INSERT INTO Employees VALUES('DW','Columbia','Gemima');
INSERT INTO Employees VALUES('HTML','Columbia','Jackson');
INSERT INTO Employees VALUES('HTML','Riffraff','Jackson');
COMMIT;
```

PROJECT	EMPLOYEE	MANAGER
Analysis	Brad	Joe
Analysis	Riffraff	Jim
Analysis	Magenta	Jim
DW	Janet	Larry
DW	Brad	Larry
DW	Columbia	Gemima
HTML	Columbia	Jackson
HTML	Riffraff	Jackson

Figure 3.37 A pre-5th normal form three-column composite primary key table.

Figure 3.38 shows the 5th normal form transformation from single three-column composite primary key table into three related tables. Also note that a PROJECT table's manager may or may not be the EMPLOYEE table's manager and that you could consider changing column names in specific tables.

Figure 3.39 shows the actual data structures that reflect 5th normal form structure shown at the bottom right of the diagram in Figure 3.38.

And next to validate the 5th normal form tables, note that all rows added are exactly the same as for adding to the pre-5th normal form table, with

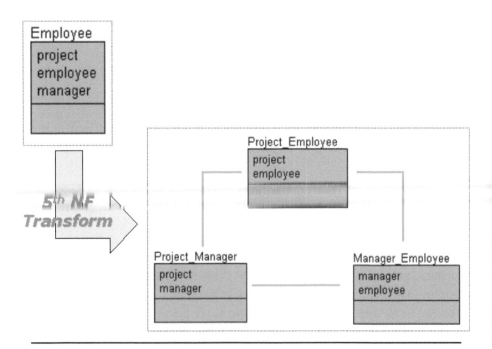

Figure 3.38 A 5th normal form transformation.

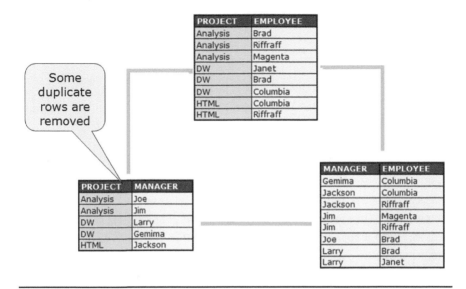

Figure 3.39 5th normal form transformations sometimes remove duplicates and prevent update anomalies.

any duplicate rows removed. Create the PROJECT_EMPLOYEE table and add rows:

```
CREATE TABLE Project_Employee
(
        project VARCHAR2(32) NOT NULL,
        employee VARCHAR2(32) NOT NULL,
        PRIMARY KEY (project, employee)
);

INSERT INTO Project_Employee VALUES('Analysis','Brad');
INSERT INTO Project_Employee VALUES('Analysis','Riffraff');
INSERT INTO Project_Employee VALUES('Analysis','Magenta');
INSERT INTO Project_Employee VALUES('DW','Janet');
INSERT INTO Project_Employee VALUES('DW','Brad');
INSERT INTO Project_Employee VALUES('DW','Columbia');
INSERT INTO Project_Employee VALUES('HTML','Columbia');
INSERT INTO Project_Employee VALUES('HTML','Riffraff');
COMMIT;
```

Create the PROJECT_MANAGER table and add rows:

```
CREATE TABLE Project_Manager
(
        project VARCHAR2(32) NOT NULL,
        manager VARCHAR2(32) NOT NULL,
        PRIMARY KEY (project, manager)
);

INSERT INTO Project_Manager VALUES('Analysis','Joe');
INSERT INTO Project_Manager VALUES('Analysis','Jim');
INSERT INTO Project_Manager VALUES('DW','Larry');
INSERT INTO Project_Manager VALUES('DW','Gemima');
INSERT INTO Project_Manager VALUES('HTML','Jackson');
COMMIT;
```

Create the MANAGER_EMPLOYEE table and add rows:

```
CREATE TABLE Manager_Employee
(
        manager VARCHAR2(32) NOT NULL,
        employee VARCHAR2(32) NOT NULL,
        PRIMARY KEY (manager, employee)
);

INSERT INTO Manager_Employee VALUES('Gemima','Columbia');
INSERT INTO Manager_Employee VALUES('Jackson','Columbia');
INSERT INTO Manager_Employee VALUES('Jackson','Riffraff');
INSERT INTO Manager_Employee VALUES('Jim','Magenta');
INSERT INTO Manager_Employee VALUES('Jim','Riffraff');
INSERT INTO Manager_Employee VALUES('Joe','Brad');
INSERT INTO Manager_Employee VALUES('Larry','Brad');
INSERT INTO Manager_Employee VALUES('Larry','Janet');
COMMIT;
```

As already stated, the one hard-and-fast rule with respect to 5th normal form is that the pre-5th normal form rows must be identical to the 5th

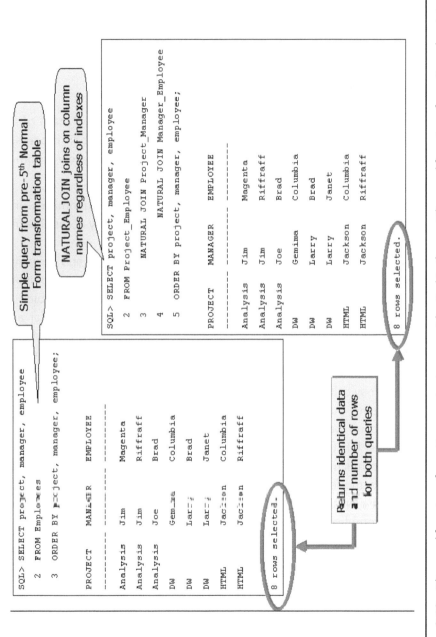

Figure 3.40 5th normal form transformations must return rows identical to the pre-5th normal form transformation when joined.

normal form divided up into tables, as shown in Figure 3.40, when querying the database. In other words, the two queries have to match—in this case rows from one table must match rows from the three joined tables, which is the case in Figure 3.40.

3.3.7.4 Domain Key Normal Form

Domain Key normal form or DKNF is quite often a conceptual state of a relational database model as opposed to a final transformation process. DKNF is the ultimate normal form and essentially describes how a completely normalized database model should appear:

- There can be no insertion, change, or data removal anomalies. In other words every row in the database must be directly accessible in all manners, such that no errors can result.
- Every row in every table must be uniquely identifiable and directly related to the primary key in its table. In other words, every column in every table is directly determined by the primary key in its table.
- All validation of data is done within the database model. As far as application and database performance are concerned, this is nearly always an extremely undesirable state in a commercial environment. It is better to split functionality between database and applications; some may call this business rules. It is generally common knowledge that some business-rule implementation is often most effectively divided up between database and applications, where the details are best left to application development coding. and avoiding placing too much of a processing burden on a database—the purpose of many modern commercial databases is storage, and imposition of structure on data and application coding is highly proficient at handling complex business rules.

DKNF is the ultimate form of relational database normalization. In an object database model this approach is perfectly suited where individual data items are only ever accessed as unique elements (primary keys) and rows are never accessed in groups. However, in a relational database model where commercially most databases require not only exact matches but also range searching for reporting, this level of intensity in normalization will have a negative impact on general database and application performance, and thus a negative effect on end-user satisfaction. End-user satisfaction is the objective of any application.

3.4 Conclusion

Application SDKs are just as powerful as database engine structural and functional capabilities. Extreme implementation of normalization using layers beyond 3rd normal form tends to place too much functionality into the database. Why not use the best of both worlds of both database and application capabilities? Use the database to store data and allow applications to manipulate and verify data to a certain extent. So before concluding in earnest, let's summarize some important points about normalization and database model design:

- What is normalization?
  - A process of removing duplication in data where removal of duplication reduces redundant (duplicated) data by splitting data into specific sections (tables).
  - Divide information into smaller, more manageable parts, but not so small as to cause performance problems.
  - Introduction of granularity to reduce redundancy and thus save space.
- What are the benefits of normalization?
  - Physical space needed to store data is reduced.
  - Data becomes better organized for usability and manageability, preferably without sacrificing performance.
  - Data accuracy and integrity.
- What are the hazards to using too much normalization?
  - Too much granularity caused by over application of normalization can result in slower retrieval of data. Very demanding concurrent OLTP databases can be very adversely affected by too much granularity. Also, end users are often non-technical, and over-granularity can tend to make table structure difficult to interpret for developers.
  - Physical space is not nearly as big a deal as it used to be, as disk space is relatively one of the lowest cost items, unless of course you are dealing with a Very Large Database (VLDB).

o More granularity tends to lead to more complexity, particularly if end users are exposed to database model structure, such as executives using a data warehouse for forecasting trends. The deeper the level of normalization the more mathematical the model becomes, making the model techie-friendly and thus very user-unfriendly. Who is accessing the database? Who will access the database in the future?

This chapter covered:

- Definitions of normalization and normal forms
- An intuitive and business-oriented method of building relational database models
- How to build tables without using normalization all the time
- Anomalies and determinants and what they mean to relational database models
- 1st, 2nd, 3rd, Boyce-Codd, 4th, Domain Key, and 5th normal forms
- How to apply normalization and normal forms by example

The next chapter will examine some advanced relational database modeling techniques, including denormalization, some special tricks used for different database model types, followed by an introduction to the object database model and data warehouse database modeling.

Chapter 4

Reading and Writing Relational Data with SQL

Any sufficiently advanced technology is indistinguishable from magic.[*]

—Arthur C. Clarke

SQL helps to explain relational database modeling;
but none of this is magic and is much easier
to understand than you might think.

This chapter shows how the relational database model is used from an application perspective. There is little point in understanding something such as relational database modeling without seeing it applied in some way, and so this chapter looks at how a database model is accessed by applications. A relational database model contains tables, where rows in tables are accessed using a computer programming language called Structured Query Language (SQL). SQL is a declarative programming language that is used to read data from tables and update data in those tables.

A declarative programming language describes what you are coding without describing how the problem is solved, which can be difficult to understand, because declarative code requires all instructions in a single complex instruction. Other computer programming languages

---

[*] https://www.brainyquote.com/quotes/arthur_c_clarke_101182

such as C and FORTRAN are procedural or modular and break software down into separate parts called *modules*; and then there is Java, which is object-oriented.

When a database model is well designed, the creation of SQL code can be a simpler process, which also can imply that difficulties encountered in coding of SQL queries can often indicate database model design flaws, or just too much granularity in a data model.

This chapter covers:

- What SQL is
- The origins of SQL
- Different types of queries
- Changing data in tables
- Changing table structure

4.1 What is SQL?

SQL is a declarative computer programming language used for accessing row and column values in relational database tables:

- SQL is structured in the sense that it is used to access structured data from tables in a relational database.
- Use of the word "language" implies a computer programming language that has specific syntax for performing specific tasks.
- SQL is a declarative language consisting of single commands where the database itself does a lot of the work in deciding how to get that information. In other words, SQL tells the database what it wants, and the database does some of the logical assessment, because logic is built into a relational database using keys and relationships between tables. A procedural language, on the other hand, contains blocks of commands, where those blocks of commands are sequences of distinct steps, typically where each successive step is dependent on the result of the previous step (command) in the sequence.
- SQL in most relational databases does have the capability to function in a limited procedural fashion, allowing the programmer to determine partially how a database is accessed. This control is given to the programmer using stored procedures, triggers, database events, or

database procedures. There are various names given to the language, and to write these code blocks depends on the database in use: Oracle calls it Programming Language/SQL (PL/SQL) and SQL Server calls it TSQL (Transact SQL). Procedural SQL inside relational databases was very simplistic years ago when it was first devised but can now be much more sophisticated, sometimes even allowing the inclusion of pro-gramming constructs such as IF statements and even object-oriented programming features. The problem with building entire applications using something like PL/SQL and TSQL is that these programming languages are built for database access, not number crunching and Graphical User Interface (GUI) manipulation and control.

So in answer to the question of what is SQL, it is a simple declarative programming language allowing single line commands where these single line commands are used to get at tables and data stored in those tables.

4.1.1 The Origins of SQL

IBM created the original relational database technology, and SQL was cre-ated as an uncomplicated, non-procedural way of accessing data from an IBM-created relational database. According to some sources, SQL was initially called "Sequel," and according to other sources SQL was initially pronounced as "ess-queue-ell." Yet further sources cite the origin of the term Sequel as being a Microsoft marketing invention in the naming of SQL Server (or Sequel Server). This is really all unimportant in the grand scheme of things as the meaning of the two pronunciations of "sequel" and "ess-queue-ell" are the same thing: SQL!

> Incidentally a query language used to access a now redundant object database called Jasmine was called Object Definitional Query Language (ODQL).

SQL in its most primitive form stems from the idea of a reporting lan-guage, which was devised in theory by the inventor of the relational data-base model. The roots of SQL lie in retrieval of sets of data, which means that SQL is intended as a language to retrieve many rows from one or many tables all at once, yielding a result set (a set of rows). SQL was originally intended to retrieve sets of rows from relational database tables and was not originally designed to retrieve individual rows from a relational database as exact row matches. On the contrary, retrieving exact matches is commonplace in transactional and OLTP databases, and modern implementations of SQL can now be used to efficiently retrieve both single rows and large sets of data.

What does all this mean without using a plethora of nasty long words? In short, SQL was developed as a shorthand method of retrieving information from relational databases, and SQL has become the industry standard over the last 20 years. Here is an example of a query (a question posed to the database that asks for specific information), which is written in SQL and retrieves all the rows in a table called AUTHOR:

```
SELECT AUTHOR_ID, NAME FROM AUTHOR;
```

4.1.2 SQL for Different Databases

SQL as implemented in different database vendor products is usually standardized using American National Standards Institute (ANSI) standardized SQL, but individual database vendors will have different naming conventions, different syntax, and even extra add-on bells and whistles. In reality, different database vendors develop a unique relational database and Relational Database Management Systems (RDBMS) containing a proprietary form of SQL.

> Relational Database Management System (RDBMS) is a term used to describe both a database and the associated tools (database management toolkit) used to work with and manage database software.

So what are the basics of SQL?

4.1.3 Introducing SQL

This section summarizes the different types of SQL as described in the following list:

- **Query Command**. Querying or reading a database is performed with a single command called the SELECT command, which is used to retrieve data from tables in a database. There are various ways in which data can be retrieved from tables:

o **Basic Query**. Retrieve all rows from a single table.

o **Filtered Query**. A filtered query uses a WHERE clause to include or exclude specific rows.

o **Sorted Query**. Sorting uses the ORDER BY clause to retrieve rows in a specific sorted order.

o **Aggregated Query**. The GROUP BY clause allows summarizing, grouping, or aggregating of rows into summarized row sets. Typically, aggregated queries contain fewer rows than the query would produce if the GROUP BY clause were not used. A HAVING clause can also be added to apply a filter to the rows produced by the GROUP BY clause. In other words the HAVING clause filters the rows produced by the GROUP BY clause, and not the rows retrieved before the GROUP BY clause is applied.

o **Join Query**. A join query joins tables together and returns rows from multiple tables. Joins can be performed in various ways, including inner joins and outer joins.

o **Nested Query**. A nested query is also known as a *subquery*, which is a query contained within a calling parent query. Nesting implies that subqueries can be nested in multiple layers, and thus a subquery itself can also be a subquery of another calling query, and so on.

o **Composite Query**. A composite query is a query that merges multiple query results together using the UNION, INTERSECT, and MINUS keywords.

• **Data Change Commands**. These commands are used to change data in tables in a database:

o **INSERT**. The INSERT command is used to add new rows to a table.

o **UPDATE**. The UPDATE command allows changes to one or more rows in a table using a single command.

o **DELETE**. The DELETE command allows deletion of one or more rows from a table using a single command.

o **MERGE or UPSERT**. This command does an INSERT and UPDATE on a group of rows at once, where a row not yet present is INSERTed, and UPDATEd if it is present.

• **Database Structure Change Commands**. These commands allow alterations to metadata, which is the data about the data; metadata in a simple relational database comprises tables and indexes. Table metadata change commands allow creation of new tables, changes to existing tables, destruction of existing tables, creation of indexes, among other more obscure types of operation types. Metadata commands used in this book include the CREATE TABLE, ALTER TABLE, DROP TABLE, and CREATE INDEX commands.

4.2 Querying a Database Using SELECT

Now let's examine database queries using the SELECT command in detail and by example. The syntax below shows the structure of the SELECT statement and the FROM clause. The SELECT list is the list of columns selected and the FROM clause specifies one or more tables to retrieve data from:

```
SELECT { [alias.]column | expression | [alias.]* [,the rest of
the list of columns] }
FROM table [alias] [ , … ];
```

The easiest way to understand SQL is by example, so retrieve all columns from the AUTHOR table using the * (star or asterisk) character:

```
SELECT * FROM AUTHOR;
```

> For the database I use, a semi-colon and carriage return is used to end the query command, submitting the query to the query engine. Not all relational databases execute on a semicolon. Some databases use a different character, others just a carriage-return.

Specify an individual column by retrieving only the name of the author from the AUTHOR table:

```
SELECT NAME FROM AUTHOR;
```

Retrieving specific column names is very slightly more efficient than retrieving all columns using the * character. This is because the * character requires the added overhead of metadata interpretation lookups into the metadata dictionary in order to find the columns in the table. In highly concurrent and very busy databases, continual data dictionary lookups can stress out database concurrency handling capacity.

Execute an expression on a single column of the AUTHOR table and return only the first ten characters of each author's name, using the SUBSTRing function:

```
SELECT AUTHOR_ID, SUBSTR(NAME,1,10) FROM AUTHOR;
```

Compute an expression, but this time involving more than a single column:

```
SELECT ISBN, (LIST_PRICE * RANK) + INGRAM_UNITS FROM EDITION;
```

> Retrieving data from tables by column names is more important for data warehouses where large portions of tables are read.

Use aliases as substitutes for table names:

```
SELECT A.NAME, P.TITLE, E.ISBN
FROM AUTHOR A JOIN PUBLICATION P ON (P.AUTHOR_ID=A.AUTHOR_ID)
JOIN EDITION E ON (E.PUBLICATION_ID=P.PUBLICATION_ID);
```

The USING clause in join syntax allows a vague specification of a join column, which assumes that the two joined tables have the required relationship on the column of the required column name. In the query above, both the AUTHOR and PUBLICATION tables have the common key column AUTHOR_ID, which links as the primary key in the AUTHOR table and a foreign key referencing an author from the PUBLICATION table and back to the AUTHOR table.

Without the aliases on the tables, the query would have table names but much longer strings, which makes the query a little more difficult to read and to code:

```
SELECT AUTHOR.NAME, PUBLICATION.TITLE, EDITION.ISBN
FROM AUTHOR JOIN PUBLICATION ON (PUBLICATION.AUTHOR_ID=AUTHOR.
AUTHOR_ID)
JOIN EDITION ON (EDITION.PUBLICATION_ID=PUBLICATION.
PUBLICATOIN_ID);
```

Using shorter alias names can help to keep SQL code more easily readable, particularly for programmers in the future having to make changes to existing code. More easily maintainable code is less prone to error and is also much easier to tune properly.

4.2.1 Filtering with the WHERE Clause

A filtered query uses the WHERE clause to include or exclude specific rows. Here is the added syntax to the SELECT command for the WHERE clause as follows:

```
SELECT …
FROM table [alias] [, … ]
[ WHERE [table.|alias.] { column | expression } comparison { …
}
[ { AND | OR } [ NOT ] … ] ];
```

The WHERE clause is optional.

Let's begin with an example filter that retrieves the author whose primary key value is equal to 2:

```
SELECT * FROM AUTHOR WHERE AUTHOR_ID = 2;
```

This filter is efficient because a single row is found using the primary key. A very fast index search can be used to find a single row very quickly, even in an extremely large table.

Now find everything other than authors whose primary key value is 2:

```
SELECT * FROM AUTHOR WHERE AUTHOR_ID != 2;
```

Filtering using a negative such as NOT or != ignores all indexes in most cases because searching for something that does not exist forces a read of all rows in the table (a full table scan). A full table scan is a physical I/O read of all the rows in a table, and reading something like an entire table containing billions of rows could take too much time. However, very small tables are more efficiently read using only the table and performing a full table scan, rather than reading index and table.

And now for authors whose primary key value is less than or equal to 2:

```
SELECT * FROM AUTHOR WHERE AUTHOR_ID <= 2;
```

A filter without equality as above would cause a range search, which is obviously less efficient than trying to find a single row. However, a range search is still more efficient than reading all the rows in a table, unless of course you want to read all the rows in a table.

This one finds another range:

```
SELECT * FROM AUTHOR WHERE AUTHOR_ID >= 2 AND AUTHOR_ID <= 5;
```

Many relational databases use a special operator called BETWEEN, which retrieves between a range that is inclusive of the end points:

```
SELECT * FROM AUTHOR WHERE AUTHOR_ID BETWEEN 2 AND 5;
```

You may have noticed the use of the AND operator in the above query. The NOT, AND, and OR operators are known as *logical operators* or *logical conditions*, depending on the database in use. Logical operators allow for Boolean logic in WHERE clause filtering and various other SQL code commands and clauses. Mathematically, the sequence of precedence is NOT, followed by AND, and finally OR. Precedence can be altered using parentheses. What is precedence?

4.2.1.1 Precedence

Precedence is the order of resolution of an expression and generally acts from left to right across an expression. In other words, in the following expression, each of the first, second, and third expressions are evaluated one after the other.

```
<expression1> AND <expression2> AND <expression3>
```

An expression is a mathematical term representing any part of a larger mathematical expression. Thus an expression is an expression in itself, it can contain other expressions, and it can be a subset part of other expressions. So in the expression:

```
( ( ( 5 + 3 ) * 23 ) - 50 )
```

(5 + 3) is an expression, (5 + 3) * 23 is an expression and so is ((5 + 3) * 23) an expression. Even the number 50 is an expression in this context.

However, in the following expression, the conjunction of the second and third expressions is evaluated first, and the result is evaluated against the first expression using the OR logical operator. This is because the AND operator has higher precedence than the OR operator:

```
<expression1> OR <expression2> AND <expression3>
```

> Higher precedence means the expression with the highest precedence is executed first.

The precedence of evaluation of expressions in the next expression is changed by using the parentheses, and so use of parentheses (round brackets) has higher precedence than NOT, AND, and OR, changing it to effectively execute the OR operator first:

```
(<expression1> OR <expression2>) AND <expression3>
```

Aside from logical operator precedence, there is also the factor of arithmetical precedence, where addition and subtraction have the lowest level of precedence, but they are equal to each other:

```
5 + 4 - 3 = 6
```

Addition and subtraction have equal precedence, because no matter in which order the numbers are added and subtracted, the result will always be the same. Try it out yourself in your head and it will make sense.

Multiplication and division have higher precedence than addition and subtraction but once again are equal in precedence to each other:

```
3 + 4 * 5 = 23 and not 35
```

Remember that parenthesizing a part of an expression changes precedence, which gives priority to the parenthesized section:

```
( 3 + 4 ) * 5 = 35
```

Any function such as raising a number to a power or using a SUBSTR function gives the functional part of the expression the highest level of precedence (also because it is parenthesized):

```
3 + 4² * 5 = 83
3 * 4 + LENGTH(SUBSTR(NAME, 1, 10)) = 22
```

> Some databases and programming languages may represent raising a number to a power in different ways, such as 4^2, 4^^2, EXP(4,2), POWER(4,2). This depends on the database in use.

Getting back to filtering, there are other ways of filtering that are common to many relational databases, such as the LIKE operator. The LIKE operator is a little like a very simple string pattern matcher where the following query finds all authors with the lowercase vowel "a" in their names:

```
SELECT * FROM AUTHOR WHERE NAME LIKE '%a%';
```

The LIKE operator is generally not efficient because a simple string pattern match character at the start of the string (in this case the % wild card character) will force a full table scan, because the string does not tell the LIKE operator exactly what string to search for.

> In computer programming lingo a wild card character is a special character that is used to find any character, or search for a pattern of one or more characters.

IN is another operator that can be used as a set membership operator:

```
SELECT * FROM AUTHOR WHERE AUTHOR_ID IN (1,2,3,4,5);
```

Traditionally, the IN operator is most efficient when testing against a list of literal values.

4.2.2 *Sorting with the ORDER BY Clause*

Sorting rows in a query requires use of the ORDER BY clause, whose syntax is as follows:

```
SELECT …
FROM table [alias] [, … ]
[ WHERE … ]
[ ORDER BY { column | expression [ASC| DESC] [ , … ] } ];
```

The ORDER BY clause is optional.

Sorting with the ORDER BY clause allows resorting to an order other than the natural physical order in which rows were originally added to a table. This first example sorts by AUTHOR_ID contained within the name of the author (the NAME column), somewhat counter intuitively thought from the inside out and known in SQL as a NAME by AUTHOR_ID sort (names sorted by authors):

```
SELECT * FROM AUTHOR ORDER BY NAME, AUTHOR_ID;
AUTHOR_ID NAME
---------- --------------------
        8 Gavin Powell
        3 Isaac Azimov
        2 James Blish
        5 Jerry Pournelle
        7 Kurt Vonnegut
        4 Larry Niven
        1 Orson Scott Card
        6 William Shakespeare
```

It is not recommended to omit the ORDER BY clause if any kind of sorted order is required but some queries will be sorted naturally without use of the ORDER BY clause, depending on data retrieved, whether tables or indexes are read and which clauses are used. Different databases have different formats for ORDER BY clause syntax, and some formats are more restrictive than others.

4.2.3 Aggregating with the GROUP BY Clause

An aggregated query uses the GROUP BY clause to summarize repeating groups of rows into aggregations or summaries of those groups. The syntax below adds the syntax for the GROUP BY clause:

```
SELECT …
FROM table [alias] [, … ]
 [ WHERE … ]
[ GROUP BY expression [, … ] [ HAVING condition ] ]
[ ORDER BY … ];
```

> The GROUP BY clause is optional to the SELECT command and the HAVING clause is an optional clause of the GROUP BY clause.

Note the sequence of the different clauses in the syntax diagram above, in that the WHERE clause is always executed first and the ORDER BY clause is always executed last. It follows that the GROUP BY clause will always appear between the WHERE clause and the ORDER BY clause.

> Some databases allow special expansions to the GROUP BY clause, allowing rollup and cubic query output, even to the point of creating highly complex spreadsheet or OLAP type analytical output.

A simple application of the GROUP BY clause can be used to create a summary, as in the following example, which creates an average price for all editions that are printed by each publisher:

```
SELECT P.NAME AS Publisher, AVG(E.LIST_PRICE)
FROM PUBLISHER P JOIN EDITION E USING (PUBLISHER_ID)
GROUP BY P.NAME;
Del Rey Books                                6.99
Berkley Publishing Group
Bantam Books                                  7.5
Fawcett Books                                6.99
Books on Tape                               29.97
Ballantine Books                            6.745
```

```
L P Books                                    23.72
Overlook Press                                34.5
Spectra                                        7.5
HarperCollins Publishers                      9.44
```

> Berkley Publishing Group has no average list price because it
> has nothing published and thus nothing for sale.

In the example above, an average price is returned for publisher, and individual editions of books are summarized into each average for each publisher. Thus individual editions of each book are not returned as separate rows because they are summarized into the averages.

The next example selects only the averages for publishers where that average is greater than 10:

```
SELECT P.NAME AS Publisher, AVG(E.LIST_PRICE)
FROM PUBLISHER P JOIN EDITION E USING (PUBLISHER_ID)
GROUP BY P.NAME
HAVING AVG(E.LIST_PRICE) > 10;
PUBLISHER                           AVG(E.LIST_PRICE)
--------------------------------    -----------------
Books on Tape                                  29.97
L P Books                                      23.72
Overlook Press                                  34.5
```

The above example filters out some of the aggregated rows using the HAVING clause, which filters GROUP BY aggregated rows (after the GROUP BY clause has been applied). A common programming error is to get the purposes of the WHERE and HAVING clause filters mixed up. The WHERE clause filters rows as they are read (as I/O activity takes place) from the database, and the HAVING clause filters aggregated groups after all database I/O activity has been completed. Do not use the HAVING clause when the WHERE clause should be used, and vice versa.

4.2.4 Join Queries

A join query is a query retrieving rows from more than one table, where rows from different tables are usually joined on related key column values.

The most efficient and effective forms of join are those between directly related primary and foreign key columns, because they should use indexes to match rows between two tables. There are a number of different types of joins:

- **Inner Join**. An intersection between two tables using matching column values, returning rows common to both tables only. Inner join syntax is as follows:

```
SELECT …
FROM table [alias] [, … ]
[
[ INNER ] JOIN table [alias]
[
    USING (column [, … ])
  | ON (column = column [{AND | OR} [NOT] [ … ])
  ]
]
[ WHERE … ] [ GROUP BY … ] [ ORDER BY … ];
```

The query below is an inner join because it finds all publishers and related published editions where the two tables are linked based on the established primary key to foreign key relationship. The PUBLISHER_ID column primary key is in the PUBLISHER table on the one side of the one-to-many relationship, which is between the PUBLISHER and EDITION tables. The foreign key is the PUBLISHER_ ID column on the many side of the one-to-many relationship in the EDITION table:

```
SELECT P.NAME AS Publisher, E.ISBN
FROM PUBLISHER P JOIN EDITION E USING (PUBLISHER_ID);
PUBLISHER                               ISBN
-------------------------------- ----------
Overlook Press                     1585670081
Ballantine Books                    345333926
Ballantine Books                    345336275
Ballantine Books                    345438353
Bantam Books                        553293362
Spectra                             553278398
```

```
Spectra                        553293370
Spectra                        553293389
L P Books                      198711905
L P Books                      893402095
Del Rey Books                  345308999
Del Rey Books                  345323440
Del Rey Books                  345334787
Books on Tape                 5553673224
Books on Tape                 5557076654
HarperCollins Publishers       246118318
Fawcett Books                  449208133
Berkley Publishing Group       425130215
```

- **Cross Join.** Also known mathematically as a *Cartesian product*, a cross join merges all rows in one table with all rows in another table, regardless of any matching values. Cross join syntax is as follows:

```
SELECT …
FROM table [alias] [, … ]
[ CROSS JOIN table [alias] ]
[ WHERE … ] [ GROUP BY … ] [ ORDER BY … ];
```

A cross-join joins two tables regardless of any relationship, and the result is a query where each row in the first table is joined to each row in the second table (a little like a merge). Cross joins are only sometimes useful because if, for example, you join two tables with 1 million rows each (10^6), then a cross join creates what is called a Cartesian product (or a cross product, with $10^6 * 10^6$ rows, which is 10^{12} rows—that is a trillion rows of data.

```
SELECT P.NAME AS Publisher, E.ISBN
FROM PUBLISHER P CROSS JOIN EDITION E;


PUBLISHER                             ISBN
--------------------------------- ----------

Berkley Publishing Group          425130215
Berkley Publishing Group          449208133
```

```
Berkley Publishing Group            553278398
Berkley Publishing Group            553293362
Berkley Publishing Group            553293370
Berkley Publishing Group            553293389
Berkley Publishing Group            893402095
Berkley Publishing Group           1585670081
Berkley Publishing Group           5553673224
Berkley Publishing Group           5557076654
Books on Tape                       198711905
Books on Tape                       246118318…
```

- **Outer join.** This join returns rows from two tables, as with an inner join, which includes both the intersection between the two tables and rows in one table that are not in the other table. Any missing values that are in one table and not the other are typically replaced with NULL values. Outer joins can be one of three forms:
  - **Left Outer Join.** All rows from the left-side table plus the intersection of the two tables where values missing from the right-side table are replaced with NULL values. Left outer join syntax is as follows:

```
SELECT …
FROM table [alias] [, … ]
[
LEFT OUTER JOIN table [alias]
[
    USING (column [, … ])
  | ON (column = column [{AND | OR} [NOT] [ … ])
  ]
]
[ WHERE … ] [ GROUP BY … ] [ ORDER BY … ];
```

This query finds the intersection between publishers and editions in addition to all publishers that currently have no titles in print:

```
SELECT P.NAME AS Publisher, E.ISBN
FROM PUBLISHER P LEFT OUTER JOIN EDITION E USING
(PUBLISHER_ID);
```

```
PUBLISHER                              ISBN
-------------------------------- ----------
Overlook Press                   1585670081
Ballantine Books                  345333926
Ballantine Books                  345336275
Ballantine Books                  345438353
Bantam Books                      553293362
Spectra                           553278398
Spectra                           553293370
Spectra                           553293389
L P Books                         198711905
L P Books                         893402095
Del Rey Books                     345308999
Del Rey Books                     345323440
Del Rey Books                     345334787
Books on Tape                    5553673224
Books on Tape                    5557076654
HarperCollins Publishers          246118318
Fawcett Books                     449208133
Berkley Publishing Group          425130215
Oxford University Press
Bt Bound
```

In the above example, any publishers with no titles currently in print have NULL valued ISBN numbers.

- o **Right Outer Join**. All rows from the right-side table plus the intersection of the two tables, where values missing from the left side table are replaced with NULL values. Right outer join syntax is as follows:

```
SELECT …
FROM table [alias] [, … ]
[
RIGHT OUTER JOIN table [alias]
[
    USING (column [, … ])
  | ON (column = column [{AND | OR} [NOT] [ … ])
```

```
       ]
   ]
   [ WHERE … ] [ GROUP BY … ] [ ORDER BY … ];
```

Now find the intersection between publishers and editions in addition to all self-published titles (the last ISBN is a self-published title because it is published by the author and has no publisher):

```
SELECT P.NAME AS Publisher, E.ISBN
FROM PUBLISHER P RIGHT OUTER JOIN EDITION E USING
(PUBLISHER_ID);
PUBLISHER                               ISBN
-------------------------------- ----------
Overlook Press                    1585670081
Ballantine Books                   345438353
Ballantine Books                   345336275
Ballantine Books                   345333926
Bantam Books                       553293362
Spectra                            553293389
Spectra                            553293370
Spectra                            553278398
L P Books                          893402095
L P Books                          198711905
Del Rey Books                      345334787
Del Rey Books                      345323440
Del Rey Books                      345308999
Books on Tape                     5557076654
Books on Tape                     5553673224
HarperCollins Publishers           246118318
Fawcett Books                      449208133
Berkley Publishing Group           425130215
                                  9999999999
```

In the above example, books without a publisher have NULL valued publishing house entries.

o **Full Outer Join.** The intersection plus all rows from the right-side table not in the left side table, in addition to all rows from the left side table not in the right side table. Full outer join syntax is as follows:

```
SELECT …
FROM table [alias] [, … ]
[
FULL OUTER JOIN table [alias]
[
    USING (column [, … ])
  | ON (column = column [{AND | OR} [NOT] [ … ])
  ]
]
[ WHERE … ] [ GROUP BY … ] [ ORDER BY … ];
```

A full outer join is not the same as a cross join.

This query finds the full outer join, which is both the left and the right outer joins at the same time:

```
SELECT P.NAME AS Publisher, E.ISBN
FROM PUBLISHER P FULL OUTER JOIN EDITION E USING
(PUBLISHER_ID);
PUBLISHER                               ISBN
-------------------------------- ----------
L P Books                               198711905
HarperCollins Publishers                246118318
Del Rey Books                           345308999
Del Rey Books                           345323440
Ballantine Books                        345333926
Del Rey Books                           345334787
Ballantine Books                        345336275
Ballantine Books                        345438353
Berkley Publishing Group                425130215
Fawcett Books                           449208133
Spectra                                 553278398
Bantam Books                            553293362
Spectra                                 553293370
Spectra                                 553293389
L P Books                               893402095
Overlook Press                          1585670081
```

```
Books on Tape                    5553673224
Books on Tape                    5557076654
                                 9999999999
Bt Bound
Oxford University Press
```

In the above example, missing entries of both publishers and editions are replaced with NULL values.

○ **Self-Join**. A self join joins a table to itself and is commonly used with a table containing a hierarchy of rows such as a family tree, which is in effect a denormalized one-to-many relationship. A self-join does not require any explicit syntax other than including the same table in the FROM clause twice, as in the following example:

```
SELECT P.NAME AS PARENT, C.NAME
FROM SUBJECT P JOIN SUBJECT C ON (C.PARENT_ID = P.SUBJECT_ID);
PARENT                NAME
----------------      --------------------
Fiction               Literature
Non-Fiction           Self Help
Non-Fiction           Esoteric
Non-Fiction           Metaphysics
Fiction               Science Fiction
Non-Fiction           Technical
Technical             Computers
Fiction               Fantasy
Fiction               Drama
Fiction               Whodunnit
Fiction               Suspense
Fiction               Poetry
Literature            Shakespearian
Literature            Modern American
Literature            19th Century American
Literature            Victorian
```

Some databases do have specific syntax for performing self-joins on hierarchical data contained in a single table.

4.2.5 Nested Queries

A nested query is a query containing one or more subqueries, where nested means that a query can be nested within a query, within another query, and so on. Some databases use the IN set operator to nest queries where one value is checked for membership in a list of values found from a subquery as in the following example:

```
SELECT * FROM AUTHOR WHERE AUTHOR_ID IN
(SELECT AUTHOR_ID FROM PUBLICATION WHERE PUBLICATION_ID IN
  (SELECT PUBLICATION_ID FROM EDITION WHERE PUBLISHER_ID IN
    (SELECT PUBLISHER_ID FROM PUBLISHER)));
```

Some databases allow you to pass a cross checking or correlation value into a subquery, as in the case below, usually an index:

```
SELECT * FROM AUTHOR WHERE AUTHOR_ID IN
(SELECT AUTHOR_ID FROM PUBLICATION WHERE AUTHOR_ID = AUTHOR.
AUTHOR_ID);
```

An alias can be used as a clearer alternative to typing out the name of the table:

```
SELECT A.* FROM AUTHOR A WHERE A.AUTHOR_ID IN
(SELECT AUTHOR_ID FROM PUBLICATION WHERE AUTHOR_ID =
A.AUTHOR_ID);
```

> A correlated subquery creates a semi-join between the calling query and the subquery by passing a key value from the calling query into the subquery, which allows a join between calling query and subquery—this may not be true for all relational databases.

Subqueries can produce single scalar values, and because equality is used here between calling query and subquery, then the calling query will cause an error if it returns more than one row:

```
SELECT * FROM AUTHOR WHERE AUTHOR_ID =
```

```
(SELECT DISTINCT AUTHOR_ID FROM PUBLICATION WHERE PUBLICATION_
ID = 1);
```

> The DISTINCT clause is used to return only the unique rows in a set
> of returned rows, where the columns in that set of returned rows
> is defined by the columns listed in the SELECT clause of a query.

Subqueries can also produce and be verified as multiple columns; in this
case "*" selects all columns and checks a set of two columns against a two-
column row set in the subquery:

```
SELECT * FROM COAUTHOR WHERE (COAUTHOR_ID, PUBLICATION_ID) IN
(SELECT A.AUTHOR_ID, P.PUBLICATION_ID
  FROM AUTHOR A JOIN PUBLICATION P
  ON (P.AUTHOR_ID = A.AUTHOR_ID));
```

The ON clause in join syntax allows specification of two columns from
different tables to join on where join columns have different names:

```
SELECT * FROM AUTHOR A JOIN COAUTHOR C ON(C.COAUTHOR_ID =
A.AUTHOR_ID);
```

4.2.6 Composite Queries

Set merge operators can be used to combine two separate queries into a
merged composite query where both queries must have the same number
of columns and datatypes for each column, all in the same sequence. However, columns do not have the same names in both tables.

```
SELECT * FROM AUTHOR
UNION
SELECT * FROM PUBLISHER;
AUTHOR_ID NAME
---------- --------------------------------
         1 Orson Scott Card
         1 Overlook Press
         2 Ballantine Books
```

```
 2 James Blish
 3 Bantam Books
 3 Isaac Azimov
 4 Larry Niven
 4 Spectra
 5 Jerry Pournelle
 5 L P Books
 6 Del Rey Books
 6 William Shakespeare
 7 Books on Tape
 7 Kurt Vonnegut
 8 Gavin Powell
 8 HarperCollins Publishers
 9 Fawcett Books
10 Berkley Publishing Group
11 Oxford University Press
12 Bt Bound
```

The query above does not produce a rational result, because normally authors and publishers should be joined, rather than just merged. Also, the first table's column names are used and the second table's column names are ignored.

4.3 Changing Data in a Database

Changes to a database can be performed using the INSERT, UPDATE, and DELETE commands. Some databases have more advanced variations on these commands, such as multiple table INSERT commands and MERGE commands (merge current and historical rows). The INSERT command allows additions to tables in a database, and its syntax is generally as follows:

```
INSERT INTO table [ ( column [, … ] ) ] VALUES ( expression [
, … ]);
```

The UPDATE command has the following syntax, allowing update of one or more columns at once; and the WHERE clause filter allows updating of one or more rows:

```
UPDATE table SET column = expression [, … ] [ WHERE ... ];
```

The DELETE command is very similar in syntax to the UPDATE command, with the WHERE filter allowing the deletion of specific rows from a table:

```
DELETE FROM table [ WHERE ... ];
```

4.3.1 Understanding Transactions

In a relational database, a transaction allows you make changes where at a later point you can choose to store the changes permanently using a COMMIT command, or remove all changes made since the last COMMIT command by using a ROLLBACK command. Also, in a multi-user environment, no other connected users can see your changes until you commit them using the COMMIT command.

You can execute multiple database change commands in sequence, such as three INSERT commands to store multiple changes to a database if a COMMIT command was executed. If you were to execute a ROLLBACK command as opposed to a COMMIT, command then the three new rows would be removed from the database. In the following script the first two new authors will be added to the AUTHOR table (they are committed), and a third author will not be added (it is rolled back):

```
INSERT INTO AUTHOR(AUTHOR_ID, NAME) VALUES(100, 'Jim Jones');
INSERT INTO AUTHOR(AUTHOR_ID, NAME) VALUES(101, 'Jack Smith');
COMMIT;
INSERT INTO AUTHOR(AUTHOR_ID, NAME) VALUES(102, 'Jenny
Brown');
ROLLBACK;
```

Blocks of commands can be executed within a single transaction where all commands can be committed at once (by a single COMMIT command) or removed from the database at once (by a single ROLLBACK command). The following script introduces the concept of a block of code in a database where blocks are used to compartmentalize sections of code. This compartmental or modular approach is not only for the purposes of transaction control (controlling how transactions are executed), but also in order to create blocks of independently executable code such as a named stored procedure:

```
BEGIN
INSERT INTO AUTHOR(AUTHOR_ID, NAME) VALUES(200, 'Jim Jones
II');
INSERT INTO AUTHOR(AUTHOR_ID, NAME) VALUES(201, 'Jack Smith
II');
INSERT INTO AUTHOR(AUTHOR_ID, NAME) VALUES(202, 'Jenny Brown
II');
COMMIT;
--error trap
EXCEPTION WHEN OTHERS THEN

        ROLLBACK;
END;
/
```

> A stored procedure is a named block of code that is stored inside a database, which can be re-executed again at a later date just by calling it (you do not have to type it all in again as in the above example).

The script above includes an error trap that is active for all commands between the BEGIN and END commands. Any error occurring between the BEGIN and END commands will reroute execution to the error-trapping section, executing the ROLLBACK command instead of the COMMIT command, and so the error-trap section aborts the entire block of code, undoing any changes made so far. Any of the INSERT commands can trigger the error-trap condition for any kind of error condition that occurs.

The previous block of code would have to be typed in again if you wanted to execute it again, but if you could store it in the database as a named stored procedure, it would look like this.

```
CREATE OR REPLACE PROCEDURE DOTHIS AS
BEGIN
INSERT INTO AUTHOR(AUTHOR_ID, NAME) VALUES(300, 'Jim Jones
III');
INSERT INTO AUTHOR(AUTHOR_ID, NAME) VALUES(301, 'Jack Smith
III');
```

```
INSERT INTO AUTHOR(AUTHOR_ID, NAME) VALUES(302, 'Jenny Brown
III');
COMMIT;
--error trap
EXCEPTION WHEN OTHERS THEN
       ROLLBACK;
END DOTHIS;
/
```

> A stored procedure is also known as a *named
> procedure* or a *database procedure.*

And then you could execute it again later on just by calling the named procedure again:

```
EXECUTE DOTHIS;
```

And you also call the DOTHIS named procedure from another block or procedure:

```
BEGIN
DOTHIS;
END;
/
```

and you can drop the procedure like this:

```
DROP PROCEDURE DOTHIS;
```

4.4 Changing Database Metadata

Database objects such as tables define how data is stored in a database, and thus database objects are known as *metadata,* which is the data about the data. In general, all databases include CREATE, ALTER, and DROP commands for most object types (not all object types can be ALTERed).

The following command would create a new table of authors called AUTHOR1:

```
CREATE TABLE AUTHOR1(
        AUTHOR_ID INTEGER NULL,
        NAME VARCHAR(32) NULL);
```

Use the ALTER TABLE command to set the AUTHOR_ID column as non-nullable:

```
ALTER TABLE AUTHOR1 MODIFY(AUTHOR_ID NOT NULL);
```

Use the DROP TABLE and CREATE TABLE commands to recreate the AUTHOR1 table with two constraints:

```
DROP TABLE AUTHOR1;
CREATE TABLE AUTHOR1 (
        AUTHOR_ID INTEGER PRIMARY KEY NOT NULL,
        NAME VARCHAR(32) UNIQUE NOT NULL);
```

Another CREATE TABLE command creates a new publication table called PUBLICATION1, which includes a foreign key (REFERENCES AUTHOR), which points back to the primary key column on the AUTHOR table:

```
CREATE TABLE PUBLICATION1(
        PUBLICATION_ID INTEGER PRIMARY KEY NOT NULL,
        AUTHOR_ID INTEGER REFERENCES AUTHOR NOT NULL,
        TITLE VARCHAR(64) UNIQUE NOT NULL);
```

A relational database should automatically create an index for a primary key or for a unique key column. This is because when adding a new row, a primary key must be checked for uniqueness, because a primary key is supposed to be unique. What better way to maintain unique key values than by using an index? However, foreign key columns can be both NULL valued and duplicated in a child table, and so foreign keys are not required to be unique. This is because a primary key to foreign key relationship can be a one-to-many relationship, which can consist of one primary key value to zero (a NULL foreign key), one or many duplications of the primary key value in the foreign key column on the child table (the many side of the one-to-many relationship). In other words, there are potentially many different publications for each author, as authors often write more than one book. In addition, a foreign key value could potentially be NULL valued, where an author does not necessarily have to have any publications currently in print. Therefore, creating an index on a foreign key column is not automatically controlled by a relational database. However, an index is usually required for a foreign key column, because of potential locking and full table scanning problems when references are checked between primary key and foreign key tables, so it is usually prudent to create foreign key indexes manually:

```
CREATE INDEX XFK_PUBLICATION_AUTHOR ON PUBLICATION1
(AUTHOR_ID);
```

Indexes can also be altered and dropped using the ALTER INDEX and DROP INDEX commands, respectively, and the new tables created temporarily above can be dropped using the DROP TABLE command, which incidentally also drops any indexes created on those tables:

```
DROP TABLE PUBLICATION1;
DROP TABLE AUTHOR1;
```

In general, database metadata change commands are a lot more comprehensive than just creating, altering, and dropping simple tables and indexes, but it is not necessary to bombard you with too much detail on metadata in this book.

Figure 4.1 shows the tables of the online bookstore database model, and as an exercise you can create all tables and also add in all primary key and foreign key constraints:

1. It is important to create the table in the correct sequence, because primary and foreign key relationships will dictate that some tables depend on the existence of others.
2. The PUBLISHER, AUTHOR, and SUBJECT tables can be created first, because they are at the top of dependency hierarchies.
3. Next create the PUBLICATION table.
4. Last of all, create the EDITION, REVIEW, and COAUTHOR tables.

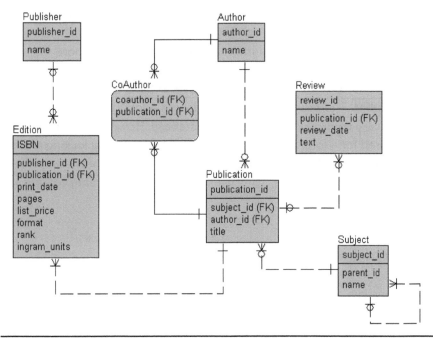

Figure 4.1 The online book store relational database model.

And the tables can be created as follows:

1. Create the PUBLISHER, AUTHOR, and SUBJECT tables (natural key names and titles should be specified as unique if not primary key columns):

```
CREATE TABLE PUBLISHER(
  PUBLISHER_ID INTEGER PRIMARY KEY NOT NULL,
  NAME VARCHAR(32) UNIQUE NOT NULL);

CREATE TABLE AUTHOR(
  AUTHOR_ID INTEGER PRIMARY KEY NOT NULL,
  NAME VARCHAR(32) UNIQUE NOT NULL);

CREATE TABLE SUBJECT(
  SUBJECT_ID INTEGER PRIMARY KEY NOT NULL,
  PARENT_ID INTEGER REFERENCES SUBJECT NULL,
  NAME VARCHAR(32) UNIQUE NOT NULL);
```

2. Create the PUBLICATION table (indexes can be created on foreign key columns):

```
CREATE TABLE PUBLICATION(
  PUBLICATION_ID INTEGER PRIMARY KEY NOT NULL,
  SUBJECT_ID INTEGER REFERENCES SUBJECT NOT NULL,
  AUTHOR_ID INTEGER REFERENCES AUTHOR NOT NULL,
  TITLE VARCHAR(64) UNIQUE NOT NULL);


CREATE INDEX XFK_P_AUTHOR ON PUBLICATION(AUTHOR_ID);
CREATE INDEX XFK_P_PUBLISHER ON PUBLICATION(SUBJECT_ID);
```

3. Create the EDITION and REVIEW tables (indexes can be created on foreign key columns). Also note that a surrogate key is not used here because the ISBN is the unique numeric International Standard Book Number code. Note that the PUBLISHER_ID on the EDITION table is NULLable because books can be self-published and have no publisher:

```
CREATE TABLE EDITION(
  ISBN INTEGER PRIMARY KEY NOT NULL,
  PUBLISHER_ID INTEGER REFERENCES PUBLISHER NULL,
  PUBLICATION_ID INTEGER REFERENCES PUBLICATION NOT NULL,
  PRINT_DATE DATE NULL,
  PAGES INTEGER NULL,
  LIST_PRICE INTEGER NULL,
  FORMAT VARCHAR(32) NULL,
  RANK INTEGER NULL,
  INGRAM_UNITS INTEGER NULL);


CREATE INDEX XFK_E_PUBLICATION ON EDITION(PUBLICATION_ID);
CREATE INDEX XFK_E_PUBLISHER ON EDITION(PUBLISHER_ID);

CREATE TABLE REVIEW(
  REVIEW_ID INTEGER PRIMARY KEY NOT NULL,
  PUBLICATION_ID INTEGER REFERENCES PUBLICATION NOT NULL,
  REVIEW_DATE DATE NOT NULL,
  TEXT VARCHAR(4000) NULL);
```

4. The COAUTHOR table introduces something new, because the primary key is a composite of two columns, and so the primary key must be created after both columns have been created, and not as each column is created:

```
CREATE TABLE COAUTHOR(
  COAUTHOR_ID INTEGER REFERENCES AUTHOR NOT NULL,
  PUBLICATION_ID INTEGER REFERENCES PUBLICATION NOT NULL,
  PRIMARY KEY(COAUTHOR_ID, PUBLICATION_ID));

CREATE INDEX XFK_CA_PUBLICATION ON COAUTHOR(COAUTHOR_ID);
CREATE INDEX XFK_CA_AUTHOR ON COAUTHOR(PUBLICATION_ID);
```

4.5 Conclusion

This chapter covered:

- What SQL is, what SQL is used for, and the origin of SQL.
- SQL is a reporting language for relational databases.
- SQL is primarily designed to retrieve sets or groups of related rows.
- SQL was not originally intended for retrieving unique rows but does this fairly well in modern relational databases.
- There are many different types of queries that are used for extracting and presenting information to the user in different ways.
- There are three specific commands: INSERT, UPDATE, and DELETE, which are used for changing rows in tables.
- Tables and indexes can be changed using table and index database metadata change commands.
- There are some very simple ways of building better written, more maintainable and faster performing SQL code commands.

Above all, this chapter has shown how the relational database model is used from an application perspective. There is little point in trying to understand something like relational database modeling without seeing it applied in some way. The next chapter will return to the topic of relational database modeling by presenting some advanced relational database modeling techniques.

Chapter 5

Advanced Relational Database Modeling

A computer lets you make more mistakes
faster than any invention in human history—
with the possible exceptions of handguns and tequila.[*]

—Mitch Ratliffe

Acts of over-zealousness in the application of normalization
techniques can be partially rectified by using denormalization,
or a data warehouse, or perhaps BigData.

This chapter expands on the concepts of relational database modeling, normalization, and normal forms by introducing the opposite of normalization, which is denormalization and data warehousing.

It is all very well understanding how to build normalized table structures, but without knowledge of how to undo those granular structures through denormalization, you will not be able to understand other essential topics of database modeling, such as how to speed up a poorly performing database or how to build a data warehouse.

---

[*] https://www.goodreads.com/author/quotes/765026.Mitch_Ratcliffe

You may wonder why this book has talked about normalization and now tells you that you should also think about undoing some of that normalized granularity. It might even be a little frustrating that this book sometimes seems to tell you to do one thing, and then to do the opposite. Data modeling is not an exact science, and normalization is a mathematical abstraction. You cannot always take a purely mathematical approach to data modeling, because in commercial environments, you will have to cut corners for practical reasons, such as performance needs, cost, and the fact that there are people that have to fix broken databases. Do not strive for perfection in a commercial environment, but rather aim for what gets the job done. Of course getting the job done could involve perfection when putting astronauts into space, but in some environments like a database, getting the best percentage return is often more important. So a perfectly normalized relational data model design is not always the most practical option.

This chapter will bridge the gap between creating properly normalized table structures that might be too granular, to ultimately creating adequately performing table structures, because good performance services applications in a usable manner—usability is all-important. Modern day applications are often built using object-oriented SDK kits, and so this chapter also includes a brief introduction to object modeling theory—a little understanding of objects is important. In addition, data warehouses are essential to stripping old data from active OLTP databases, and also so that good projections and forecasting facilities can be provided to management and leadership level end users. Therefore, an introduction to data warehousing is included here as a primer for further detail in the next chapter.

This chapter covers:

- Denormalization
- Denormalization by reversing of normal forms
- Denormalization using specialized database objects
- The object database model
- The data warehouse database model

Let us begin this chapter by examining the topic of denormalization.

5.1 Understanding Denormalization

What is denormalization? Denormalization is often, but not always, the opposite of normalization. Denormalization can be applied to a database model in order to create data warehouse or reporting-only type tables. Denormalization is also sometimes required as a solution to revive dying OLTP applications that have poor performance as a result of over normalization and too much granularity in a data model—it is usually a last chance measure to change underlying tables, as application code would have to be changed as well, which is probably extensive and is always expensive. In fast-paced and demanding commercial environments, too much granularity in normalized data models can cause as many problems as it solves, and so denormalization will often attempt to reverse granularity, created by over-application of normal forms applied during normalization of a data model.

Denormalization is often a reversal of the processing performed by normalization, and so to begin with, let us go through a quick reminder of the accepted normal forms in normalization, followed by my more intuitive form of relational data model design.

5.1.1 Normal Form Definitions

These are the normal forms as defined by the accepted form of relational data model design normalization:

- **1st Normal Form (1NF).** Eliminate repeating elements or groups of elements within a table where each row in the table relies on and is identified uniquely by the primary key.
- **2nd Normal Form (2NF).** All non-key values must be fully functionally dependent on the primary key, such that no partial dependencies are allowed.

You would never denormalize 1st or 2nd normal forms in the name of performance for an OLTP database, but anything beyond that is a candidate for denormalization. Note that this type of denormalization may apply in a data warehouse, but possibly more likely in a BigData database.

- **3rd Normal Form (3NF)**. Transitive dependencies are not allowed, in that one column that does not depend on the primary key instead depends on a second column that does depend on the primary key.
- **BCNF or Boyce-Codd Normal Form**. Every determinant in a table is a candidate key, but if there is only one candidate key, then 3rd normal form and Boyce-Codd normal form are the same thing.
- **4th Normal Form**. Eliminate multiple sets of multi-valued dependencies.
- **5th Normal Form (Projection Normal Form)**. Eliminate cyclic dependencies.
- **DKNF or Domain Key Normal Form**. DKNF is the ultimate application of normalization and a measurement of conceptual state as opposed to a final transformation process.

> Normalization describes the key, the whole key,
> and nothing but the key.

5.1.2 Intuitive Data Modeling Definitions

These are my intuitive steps of relational data model granularization:

- **Master-Detail Relationship**. Remove repeating columns by creating a new table where the original table and the new table are linked together with a master-detail, one-to-many relationship (the original table is the master table, with fewer columns).
- **Dynamic-Static Relationship**. Perform a seemingly similar function as that described for a master-detail relationship, but in this case create a new table where repeating *values* rather than repeating *columns* are removed to the new table. The result is a many-to-one relationship rather than a one-to-many relationship created between the original table and the new table.
- Again, like 1st and 2nd normal form, you would never denormalize master-detail or dynamic-static relationships in the name of performance for an OLTP database; but anything beyond that is a candidate for denormalization.
- **Many-to-Many Join Resolution Entity**. Two entities with a many-to-many relationship is resolved with a new table. The new table connects to the two original tables with two many-to-one relationships.

> A many-to-many join resolution entity is also known as an associative entity because it associates two things with each other correctly.

- **Amalgamating Duplication from More than One Table.** If the same data is repeated in two static tables, then those shared columns can be moved to a new, shared table.
- **Splitting off a Transitive Dependency.** This is a case where a column (column B) is dependent on the non-primary key (column A) in the same table, where only column A is dependent on the primary key of the table. The new table contains the first column (column A) as its primary key along with column B.
- **Removing a Calculated Value.** Calculated values that are dependent on other columns in the same table can be removed altogether, because they can be recalculated. This is a special case of transitive dependence because a calculated value is indirectly dependent on the primary key.
- **One-To-One NULL Table.** When a column in a table is often NULL, then that column can be moved to a new table because it only depends on the primary key when it is not NULL.

5.1.3 Denormalizing Granularity Created in Chapter 3

It is normal to normalize and then denormalize later on if performance demands it. Figure 5.1 shows reversal of the normalization processing applied in Figure 3.21, where removing nullable columns to separate tables is a common process that is used to save space.

Figure 5.2 shows reversal of normalization processing applied in Figure 3.32, showing an application of BCNF where all candidate keys are separated into separate tables. A candidate key is any column that can potentially be used as a primary key (unique identifier) for the original entity—in this case a customer (the CUSTOMER table). Applying this type of normalization in a commercial environment can result in poor performance.

Figure 3.38 showed a 5th normal form transformation to remove cyclic dependencies. It might be better to place this type of layering into application coding, leaving the EMPLOYEE table as it is and denormalizing as shown in Figure 5.3. So the EMPLOYEE table would retain the project,

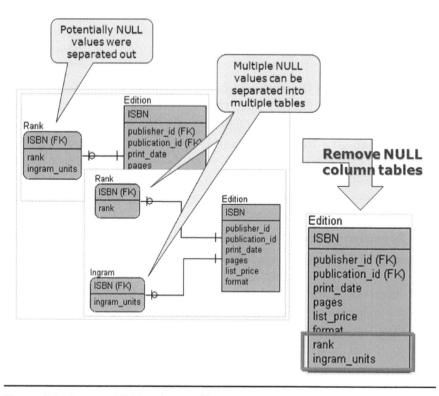

Figure 5.1   Remove NULL column tables.

manager, and employee names, and queries can use WHERE clause filtering to find the correct rows as required.

The role of 3rd normal form is to eliminate what are called *transitive dependencies.* A transitive dependency is where a column is not directly determined by the primary key, but indirectly determined by the primary key through another column.

> Most of the normal form layers beyond 3rd normal form are often impractical in a commercial environment because applications can often do a better job with programming code. What happens in reality is that 3rd normal form occupies a gray area, fitting in between what should not be commercially applied in the database model (beyond 3rd normal form), and what should definitely be left to the database model (1st, 2nd, and 3rd normal form).

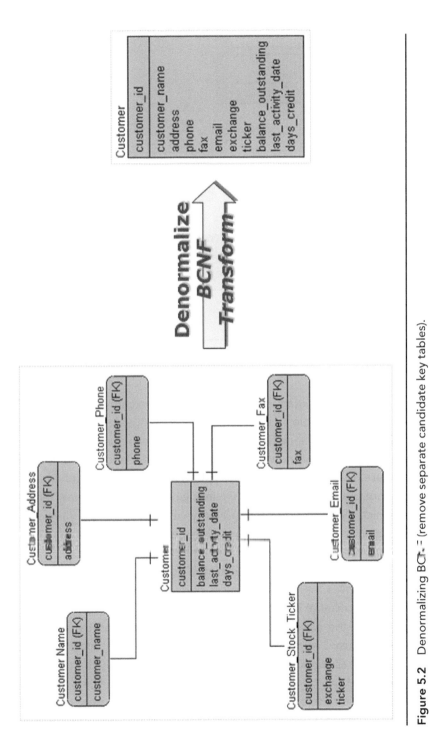

Figure 5.2 Denormalizing BCNF (remove separate candidate key tables).

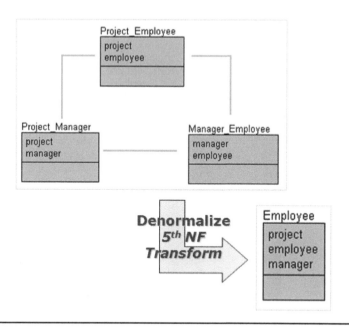

Figure 5.3   Denormalization of 5th normal form cyclic dependencies.

Figure 5.4 shows amalgamated columns where the common columns are extracted into a new table as shown in Figure 3.16. Again, too much granularity is typically a hindrance to commercial performance requirements.

Figure 5.5 shows the removal of a transitive dependency resolution created in Figure 3.17. Once again, the transformation provides mathematical precision, but practical commercial value is lacking because a new table is created, which will probably contain a very small number of columns and rows. The gain in disk space will very likely be outweighed by the loss in performance as a result of bigger joins in queries.

Figure 5.6 shows a removal of calculated columns performed in Figure 3.18, which removes a total value that is derived from two columns in the same table. The value of including the total amount on each row containing the elements of the expression as well can be determined by how much a total value is used at the application level. Also, if the constituents of the totaling expression are not required, then perhaps only the total value should be stored.

Dynamic static relationships are created by adding a new table containing static data and removing repeated static values from transactional

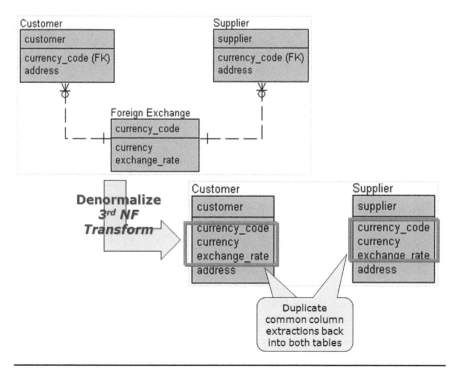

Figure 5.4   Removal of amalgamated columns in an extra table.

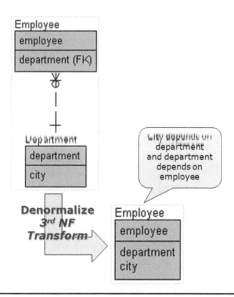

Figure 5.5   Denormalization of a transitive dependence resolution table.

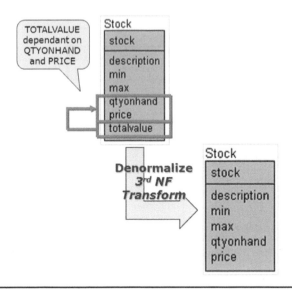

Figure 5.6   Removal of calculated columns.

tables. Figure 5.7 shows an example of over application of dynamic-static relationships where everything that can be separated out has been separated out. The top left of the diagram in Figure 5.7 shows an extreme example of four tables, created from what is essentially a more than adequately normalized COMPANY table at the bottom right of Figure 5.7.

5.1.4 Denormalization Using Specialized Database Objects

Many databases have specialized database objects for certain types of tasks. There are some specialized objects that allow for physical copies of data that can be used to transform data into a denormalized form:

- **Materialized Views**. Materialized views are allowed in many larger relational databases and are commonly used in data warehouses for pre-calculated aggregation queries. The result is less I/O activity by direct access to aggregated data that is stored in materialized views, because aggregated materialized views will typically contain far fewer rows than underlying tables, reducing I/O activity and increasing performance.

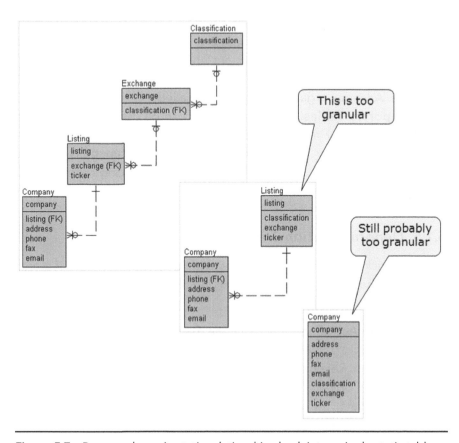

Figure 5.7   Remove dynamic-static relationships back into a single static table.

Views are overlays that can read underlying tables. Materialized views create copies of data and do not read underlying tables when queried. Materialized views can be better for performance in large databases, but reading views can be just as efficient as reading tables, but depending on the sophistication of the database vendor.

- **Clusters**. These objects allow physical copies of heavily accessed columns and tables in join queries, allowing for faster access to data with more precise I/O.

- **Index-Organized Tables**. A table can be constructed including both index and data columns built into the same physical space. The table itself becomes both the index and the data, since the table is constructed as a sorted index, as opposed to a heap of unorganized data. An index organized table is also called a *clustered index.*
- **Temporary Tables**. Temporary tables can be used on a temporary basis either for a connected session or for a period of time. Typically, temporary tables perform intermediary functions, helping to eliminate duplication or processing and reducing repetitive I/O activities.

5.1.5 Denormalization Tricks

There are tricks to denormalizing data that do not involve reversal of granularity, denormalization, or use of specialized objects. These are some ideas to consider:

- **Separate Active and Inactive Data**. Data can be separated into separate physical tables or partitions in order to separate active and inactive tables. Retaining archived and active data in the same physical space can drastically decrease performance to the most frequently needed data, the active data—because inactive data becomes so much larger than active data after an extended period of time.

> Separation of active and inactive data is the purpose of a data warehouse, where the data warehouse contains the inactive data, which is removed from the operational customer-facing OLTP environments and can dramatically increase performance.

- **Copy Columns Between Tables**. Make copies of columns between tables not directly related to each other. This can help to avoid multiple table joins between two tables where other tables must be *passed through* in order to join the two desired tables. An example is shown in Figure 5.8, where the SUBJECT_ID column is duplicated into the EDITION table to avoid joining EDITION, PUBLICATION, and SUBJECT tables, to allow access to related EDITION and SUBJECT table entries.

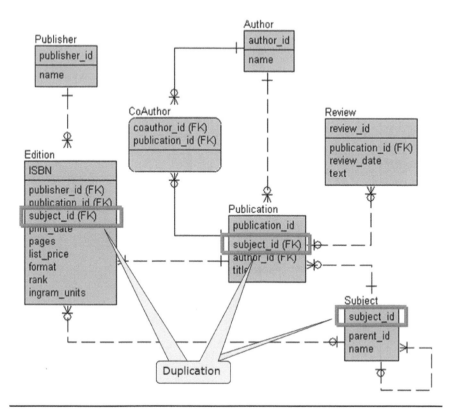

Figure 5.8   Denormalize by copying columns to reduce join sizes.

- **Summary Columns in Parent Tables**. This can help to avoid costly grouping joins, but real time updates can cause serious problems with hot blocks. Examples are shown in Figure 5.9.

> A hot block is a very busy part of the database accessed much too often by many different sessions, and all at the same time.

- **Separate Heavily and Lightly Accessed Columns**. Much like separating inactive and active data at the table level, tables containing columns with vastly different rates of access can be separated. This avoids continual physical scanning of rarely used data column values, especially when those values contain a lot of NULLs.

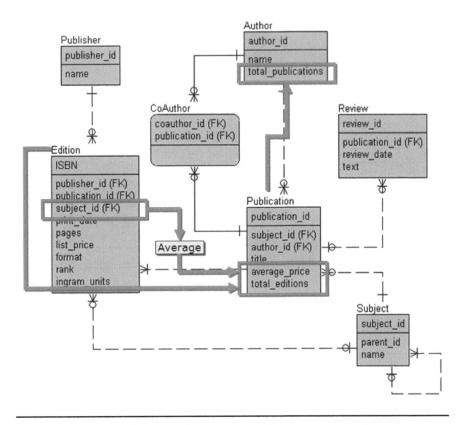

Figure 5.9　Denormalization using summary columns in parent tables.

The next general topic area examines object methodology and object-relational database aspects.

5.2　Understanding the Object Database Model

Three good reasons for including a brief description of object modeling in a book covering relational data modeling are: (1) many modern relational databases are in fact object-relational databases (a relational database allowing certain object characteristics); (2) many front-end applications are built using object-oriented programming languages (SDKs) such as Java, and those SDKs will influence and be influenced by their underlying databases; (3) BigData databases are sometimes related to and have object structured elements contained within them, which you will read about in Chapter 8. So what are the parts making up the object model?

- **Class**. A class is the equivalent of a table in a relational database.
- **Object**. An object is the iteration of a class at runtime, such that multiple object instances can be created from a class. So an object is vaguely equivalent to a row in a relational table.
- **Attribute**. An attribute is the equivalent of a relational database table column.
- **Method**. A method is equivalent to a relational database stored procedure, except that a method executes on the data contents of an object, within the bounds of that object.

In the relational database model, relationships are established using both table structures (metadata) and data values in columns, as well as those between primary and foreign key values. On the contrary, in an object database, relationships are established solely through the structure of objects and the metadata relationships between objects, which are declared by the classes defining those objects. Class collections and inheritance define an object database structure where classes are defined as containing collections of pointers to other classes, as being inherited from classes above in a hierarchy, or as being abstractions of classes below in a hierarchy. Therefore, a class can be specialized or abstracted. A specialized class is a specific form of a class, inheriting everything from its parent class, allowing local overriding changes and additions. An abstracted class is a generalized or generic form of a class containing common aspects of inherited classes.

It is important to reiterate the distinct difference between a class and an *object*. An object exists at run time. A class in an object database is a metadata structure, and objects are created from classes at run time. As a result, the structure of classes can often be different from the structure of objects created from a class hierarchy. Object database models are often designed incorrectly, because the difference between a class and an object is misunderstood. In general, class structure will never look like an object structure, because class structure is an abstraction of object structure. In addition, a class structure will not look

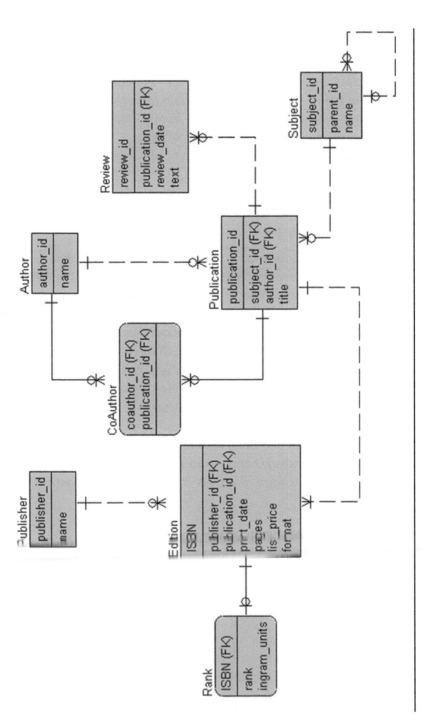

Figure 5.10 Comparing a relational database model with an equivalent object model as shown in Figure 5.11.

anything like a relational database model table structure, and if it does you might be attempting to build an object database structure into a relational database model, or visa versa, which will have poor results.

Figure 5.10 shows a relational database model that is reorganized into an object database model as shown in Figure 5.11.

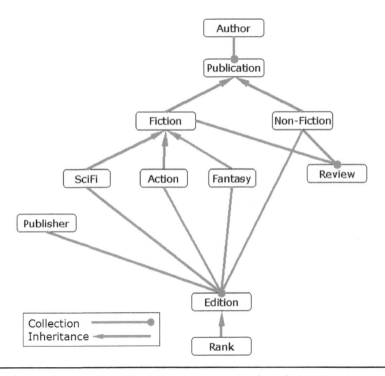

Figure 5.11   Comparing an object database model with a relational model as shown in Figure 5.10.

There are a number of differences between the relational structure shown in Figure 5.10 and the object structure shown in Figure 5.11:

- The object model has no types; the SUBJECT is an example of a type. Subjects in the BOOKS relational model are represented by both parent and child SUBJECT table rows shown by the self join displayed in Figure 5.12.

PARENT	CHILD
	Fiction
	Non-Fiction
Business	Computers
Fiction	Drama
Fiction	Fantasy
Fiction	Literature
Fiction	Poetry
Fiction	Science Fiction
Fiction	Suspense
Fiction	Whodunnit
Literature	19th Century American
Literature	Modern American
Literature	Shakespearian
Literature	Victorian
Non-Fiction	Business
Non-Fiction	Esoteric
Non-Fiction	Metaphysics
Non-Fiction	Self Help

Figure 5.12   The SUBJECT table contains a parent-child hierarchy.

The FICTION and NON-FICTION classes in the object model are representative of the SUBJECT.PARENT_ID columns. The SCIFI, ACTION, and FANTASY classes are genres, which represents three different fiction type subjects. All of these new classes are specializations of the PUBLICATION class, or more specifically, the FICTION and NON-FICTION classes are specializations of the PUBLICATION class; and the SCIFI, ACTION, and FANTASY classes are specializations of the FICTION class. Inheritance defines that objects can both contain and override aspects that are inherited from abstracted parent class definitions.

- The relationships between the different classes in the object model are represented in the class structure itself, those relationships being both collection inclusion and inheritance between classes. Collection inclusion means that runtime objects instantiated from classes contain objects containing pointers to other contained objects. Inheritance means that objects can both contain and override aspects inherited from abstracted parent class definitions.

- An invisible difference is the power of self-contained (black-box) processing using methods in an object database. Relational database stored procedures can perform a similar function to methods, but they are far more prone to human error, because stored procedures are modular and thus not black-boxed—programming code gets much more complicated when you can connect multiple modules together because it can create a complex plethora of interdependencies. Method processing can act on each class, within the scope of each class alone, so technically you only have to check each class within its own scope when testing software. This means that the removal of connections between classes makes the coding and testing much less time consuming, because there are fewer dependencies.

5.3 Introducing the Data Warehouse Model

A data warehouse model looks a little bit more real world and business oriented than an OLTP normalized data model. Where does the data warehouse model fit? When comparing the data warehouse and the relational models, the relational model is too granular for most data warehouses because the relational model introduces granularity by removing duplication, which results in a database model that is effective for front-end real-time application performance (OLTP databases). OLTP databases involve small amounts of data accessed frequently and at the same time (concurrently) by many users—many disk seeks with small disk scan. On the other hand, data warehouses require throughput of huge amounts of data by a small user population that generally runs reports and performs enormous amounts of I/O activity over millions, if not billions, of rows (it is often acceptable for data warehouse reports to take hours to run)— few disk seeks with large contiguous scans.

The heart of many data warehouses is a highly denormalized structure consisting of preferably only two distinct hierarchical layers: (1) a central table contains highly denormalized transactional data, and (2) a second layer contains referential static data. This data warehouse database model is known as the *dimensional model, fact-dimensional model,* or *star schema.*

A data warehouse consists of facts and dimensions, which are two different types of tables. Each data warehouse structure consists of a single fact table surrounded by multiple dimensions. It is possible to have more than a single fact table, but different fact tables could be related to the same set of dimension tables. Therefore, different fact tables represent an entire new set of tables that is another subset of the data warehouse, also known as a *data mart*.

> The term *data mart* is used to describe a self-contained subsection of a data warehouse.

Fact and dimension tables contain different types of data, whereas dimensions contain static data and facts contain transactional data. Transactional data is a company's daily activities, such as sales made to its customers. The dimensions describe the facts, such as the customer's name and address. For example, an online retailer selling thousands of items per day could ship one hundred items to each customer every year. Over the course of a number of years, each customer might be shipped hundreds of separate items. The detail information about a customer such as their address is relatively static information (static information does not change very often). Also, the customer is a dimension because the customer dimension describes the facts, or the transactions (a customer describes some static detailed information about each sales made to each customer).

An active OLTP database may have all older transactions deleted from its active files on a periodical basis—annually for instance. Annual historical data could then be archived into a data warehouse, and that resulting data warehouse data can then be used for forecasting (making guesses as to what customers might purchase over the next 10 years). The result of all this mishmash of complicated activities and other wonderful stuff is a table structure looking something like that shown in Figure 5.13, which shows a useful-to-table structure, describing graphically what is known as a *star schema* (a single fact table surrounded by a layer of unrelated dimensions in the form of a star). Data warehouse models can be made up of multiple data marts (subset star schemas).

> Not all data warehouses are star schemas and some are 3rd normal form. Some data warehouses contain both star schemas and 3rd normal form tables.

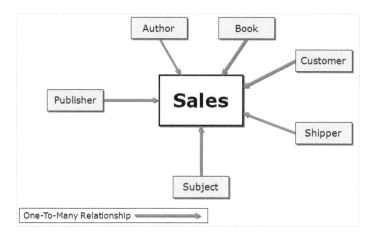

Figure 5.13   A data warehouse model star schema.

In Figure 5.13, dimensions are PUBLISHER, AUTHOR, BOOK, SUBJECT, CUSTOMER, and SHIPPER tables. The single fact table is the SALES table, and it is surrounded by a star format (star schema) by multiple dimensions. Each dimension is related to the single fact table through a one-to-many relationship.

5.4 Conclusion

This chapter covered:

- Denormalization
- Denormalization using reversal of normal forms created by normalization
- Denormalization using specialized database objects such as materialized views
- The object database model
- A brief introduction to the data warehouse database model

This chapter has described some advanced database modeling topics, including denormalization, a brief description of object database modeling followed by data warehouse modeling. A brief grasp of object modeling is important to understanding the basics of object-relational databases and some parts of the BigData field, as well as how object-built applications will interact with relational databases. Denormalization is essential to understanding database performance as well as the topic of data warehousing database modeling. Data warehousing is very important to modern day databases for reporting and trend analysis and is a large topic in itself, and so the next chapter covers data warehouse database modeling in detail.

Chapter 6

Understanding Data Warehouse Database Modeling

Intuition becomes increasingly valuable in the new information society precisely because there is so much data.[*]

—John Naisbitt

Data warehouses need special treatment and a special type of approach to database modeling, simply because they can get so unmanageably large.

The previous chapter introduced the data warehouse database model in addition to other advanced relational database modeling techniques, briefly comparing data warehouse modeling relative to both the relational and object database models. This chapter will now delve deeply into the details of the database warehouse database model, including the different types of schemas and components and how they fit together.

Expanding the relational database model to include the data warehouse database model is important because in the modern computerized world, there are a lot of data warehouse database installations in existence, and some of those data warehouses are very big. When things get bigger, they

---

[*] https://www.brainyquote.com/quotes/john_naisbitt_159130

have a habit of getting more expensive to build and maintain, even sur-
passing the cost of a source OLTP transactional database in some cases. So
describing data warehouse data modeling is just as important as describing relational database modeling for OLTP and transactional databases.

This chapter covers:

- The origin of data warehouses
- Data warehouses and their specialized database models
- Star and snowflake schemas
- Facts and dimensions
- The fact-dimensional database model
- How to build a data warehouse database model
- The contents of a data warehouse database and model

6.1   What Is a Data Warehouse?

Data warehouses were originally devised because existing databases were
being subjected to conflicting requirements, where conflict arose between
operational use and decision support requirements as follows:

- **Operational Use.** Operational use of a database requires a precise,
  accurate, and instant picture of data in a database, including all day-
  to-day operations in the functional running of a business. When a
  customer comes through the door and requests a specific part for a
  specific automobile for a specific year, that part is searched for in a
  database. Once the customer makes the purchase, they are invoiced;
  the customer pays, and the transaction is processed through bank
  accounts or otherwise. All of this is operational type activity on small
  amounts of data, and the response needs to be instantaneous (real
  time)—you want to keep the customer from waiting. So the operational aspect of a company is the heart of its business, bringing in
  daily sales and revenue.
- **Decision Support Use.** Where operational use divides data based
  on business function, decision support requires division of database
  data based on subject matter. Operational use requires access to
  specific items, such as a specific part for a specific automobile, and
  decision support use requirements might be a summary of which
  parts were ordered on which dates (the customer is not included). A

decision support database presents reports such as all parts in stock plus all parts ordered, and perhaps over the period of a whole year. The result could be a projection of when new parts should be ordered or what types of parts sell where. This allows company employees to more efficiently restock popular items and for executives to make high-level business decisions based on potential trends in sales.

So there is a big difference between requirements for operational and decision support databases: (1) operational systems require instant responses on small amounts of information, and (2) decision support systems need access to large amounts of data. The invention of data warehouses was inevitable in order to reduce conflict between operational OLTP databases and the large disk access requirements of reporting.

The demands of the modern global economy and the Internet dictate that end-user operational applications are required to be active 24x7, 365 days a year—constantly! There is no window for any type of batch activity, because when people are asleep in Europe, others are awake down under in Australia. The global economy requires instant and acceptable servicing of the needs of a global user population, otherwise your customers will go elsewhere and you will not make any money.

In reality, the most significant difference between OLTP databases and data warehouses extends all the way down to the storage layer. OLTP databases need highly efficient sharing of critical memory resources and have very specific, but also small and random, I/O requirements. Data warehouses are completely the opposite and need less sharing of memory resources, but they do consume huge amounts of CPU time and I/O bandwidth. In fact, because of the conflicting RAM and I/O requirements, placing an OLTP database and data warehouse on the same server could be highly detrimental to the success of a business.

OLTP databases need heavy resource sharing among lots of users, and data warehouses need to use those same resources for extended periods of time, which is why data warehouses exist, because the two functions can cause debilitating conflict among CPU, RAM, and I/O resources. OLTP databases generally require concurrency, which equates to heavy CPU and RAM use with low disk usage. Data warehouses require heavy CPU and disk usage, but not heavy RAM use.

6.1.1 The Relational Database Model and Data Warehouses

The traditional OLTP (transactional) type of relational database model does not cater to reporting and DSS or data warehouse requirements because the OLTP model is too granular. Granular implies too many little pieces, and the processing through all those little-bitty pieces is too time consuming for the large transactions that are typical of a DSS database. Data warehouses are all about I/O throughput and processing of huge amounts of data for relatively very few users. And even though data warehouses regularly have data added to them as batch operations, they are not normally updated because of the cost in time and resources. OLTP databases can be altered and manipulated much more easily, as they are designed for a constant stream of small adjustments from a very large group of users. So a data warehouse database simply cannot cope using a standard OLTP database relational database model, and thus something else is needed for a data warehouse.

6.1.1.1 Surrogate Keys in a Data Warehouse

Surrogate keys are replacement key values, which usually make database access more efficient. In data warehouse databases, surrogate keys are possibly more important in terms of gluing together data, because that data can often come from multiple disparate and even unrelated sources, perhaps even databases from different vendors, such as Oracle®, SQL Server, or DB2. Surrogate keys can be used to create common keys for data from different sources that might be formatted differently but mean the same thing, such as the same customer with slightly differently formatted names. For example, the human brain interprets Oracle Corp., Oracle Corporation, and ORACLE CORP. as the same thing—but a computer program will see them as three different companies. So when adding transactions to a data warehouse fact table, you will want them looking at a single definition for the same customer, and a surrogate key on the dimension containing your customers is an effective solution for linking data for the same client together, no matter how each source database spells the name of the client.

Sometimes customers could be keyed on things other than the customer's name, such as the name of a contact or even a phone number for a customer, or perhaps some kind of coding regimen such as a stock ticker (ORCL for Oracle Corporation and MSFT for Microsoft Corporation). All three of these definitions identify exactly the same customer, but if a single company is to have meaningful data from multiple sources of data, then there needs to be a common thread or key that identifies the same customer. There will only be a single row in the customer dimension table of a data warehouse for each customer; otherwise you cannot link the facts (transactions) for a customer to a single customer. A surrogate key is the perfect solution in that it uses the same surrogate key value for each iteration of the same customer.

> Some data warehouses have multiple versions of the same dimension, where older dimensional information must be retained—the medical industry is a good example.

6.1.1.2 Referential Integrity in a Data Warehouse

Data warehouse data modeling is a simpler form of relational database modeling, and referential integrity is usually only partially enforced—or not enforced at all—but might include inactive only primary and foreign key indexes for modeling purposes only. There is a certain amount of cross checking that goes on internally in a database like Oracle in order to verify relationships between primary and foreign key values when data is changed, which can be very time consuming. It is very important to understand that a data warehouse database generally has two distinct activities: (1) mass insertions of large numbers of rows, which are added en masse something like once a day; and (2) mass reads to produce reports or analytical data. It is always best to only add or remove data in a data warehouse, unless the data warehouse is under development and it cannot be avoided. The fact is that changes to existing rows are much slower than any other operation (inserts, deletes, or reads), and data warehouse physical size gets highly inhibitive to updates because updates will most likely change many small pieces, which in a very large data store can result in an overwhelming quantity of small changes.

> Some modern data warehouse databases do not have indexes at all, or even the ability to create those indexes. The reason for this is because very large data warehouses and BigData databases perform best using horizontal and vertical partitioning with pruning applied by filtering, full scanning large table objects only, making indexes completely redundant.

So now we know the origin of data warehouses and why they were devised. What is the data warehouse dimensional database model?

6.2 The Dimensional Database Model

A standard normalized relational database model can be completely unsuitable for a data warehouse, and sometimes even a denormalized relational database model might not make sense. An entirely different modeling technique is often needed for data warehouses, and it is called a *dimensional database model.* A dimensional model contains two types of tables: facts that grow quickly and dimensions that can remain relatively static over time. A fact table contains historical transactions, and dimensions describe those facts. For example, facts are all invoices issued to all customers for the last five years, which could be huge amounts of data for a large organization; dimensions will be the names and addresses for your customers.

The easiest way to describe the dimensional model is to demonstrate by example. Figure 6.1 shows a relational table structure for both static

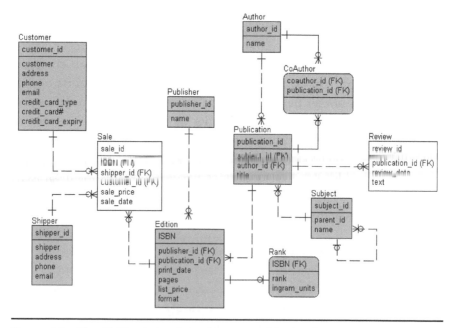

Figure 6.1   The OLTP relational database model for books.

book data (dimensions) and dynamic-transactional (facts) book data. The white tables in Figure 6.1 are transactional fact tables that change all the time, and the other tables are static data tables that do not change nearly as much.

6.2.1 What Is a Star Schema?

The most effective result for a data warehouse database model using dimensions and facts can be what is called a *star schema.* Figure 6.2 shows a simple star schema for the REVIEW fact table shown in Figure 6.1.

Figure 6.3 shows a star schema structure that is a less busy version of the diagram shown in Figure 6.2.

So what is a star schema? A star schema contains a single fact table plus a number of small dimensional tables. If there is more than one fact table, then effectively there is more than one star schema. The terminology for each star schema or fact table within a data warehouse is a data mart. Fact tables contain transactional records, which over a period of time

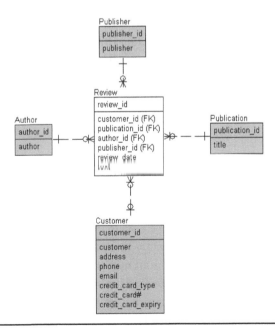

Figure 6.2   The REVIEW table fact-dimensional structure.

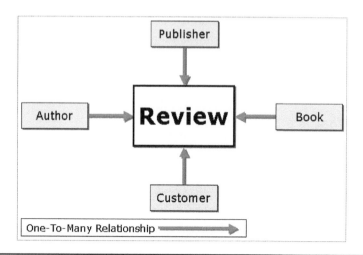

Figure 6.3   The REVIEW fact-dimensional structure is a star schema.

can eventually contain very large amounts of data. Dimension tables, on the other hand, remain relatively constant in size depending on the industry, where some industries such as the medical industry may require multiple versions of dimensions (facts are historical, and multiple versions are irrelevant and inherent in those facts). The objective is to enhance SQL query join performance for joins executed between a single fact table and multiple dimensions, all on a single hierarchical level. So a star schema is a single-level dimensional hierarchy that contains a single very large fact table, which is connected directly to each of the dimensional tables.

6.2.2 What Is a Snowflake Schema?

A snowflake schema is shown in Figure 6.4, which is a normalized star schema except that only dimension entities are normalized. Normalized dimensions have all duplication removed from each dimension, where a single fact table is connected directly to some of the dimensions (the topmost layer in the dimensional hierarchy), and thus not all of the dimensions are connected directly to the fact table. In Figure 6.4 the dimensions are grayed out in two shades of gray: the lighter shade of gray represents dimensions connected directly to the fact table (BOOK, AUTHOR, SUBJECT, SHIPPER, and CUSTOMER). The darker shaded gray dimensional

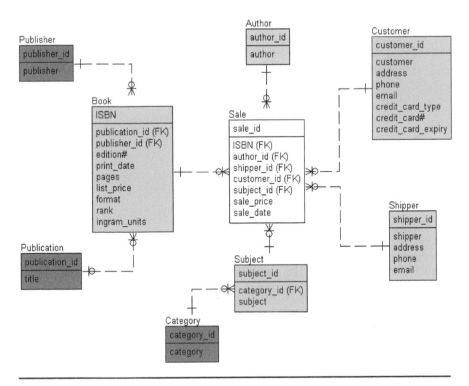

Figure 6.4   The SALE table fact-dimensional structure.

tables are normalized subset dimensional tables and are not connected to the fact table directly (PUBLISHER, PUBLICATION, and CATEGORY).

Once again, a more simplistic equivalent diagram to that of Figure 6.4 is shown by the snowflake schema in Figure 6.5.

The problem with snowflake schemas is not that there are too many tables, but rather there are too many layers. Data warehouse fact tables can become incredibly large, containing millions, billions, or even trillions of rows. The critical factor in creating star and snowflake schemas is in decreasing the number of tables in SQL query joins because fact tables are so large. The more tables in a join, then the more complex a query and the slower it will execute.

One solution is to convert (denormalize) a normalized snowflake schema into a star schema as shown in Figure 6.6, where the PUBLISHER and PUBLICATION tables have been denormalized into the BOOK table, and the CATEGORY table has been denormalized into the SUBJECT table.

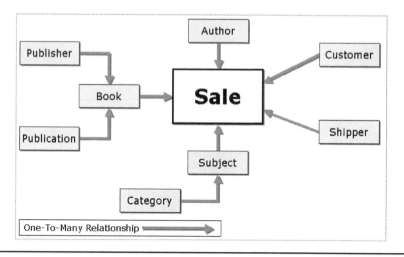

Figure 6.5   The SALE fact-dimensional structure as a snowflake schema.

And once again, a more simplistic equivalent diagram to that shown in Figure 6.6 is shown by the star schema in Figure 6.7.

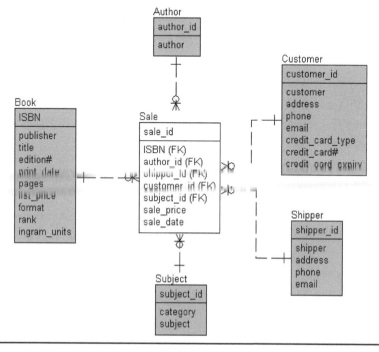

Figure 6.6   A denormalized SALE table fact-dimensional structure.

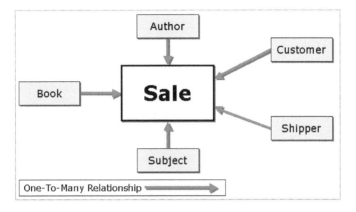

Figure 6.7   The SALE fact-dimensional structure denormalized into a star schema.

What does all this prove? Two things are achieved by using fact-dimensional structures and star schemas:

- Figure 6.1 shows a highly normalized table structure, which is useful for high concurrency and precision searches required for an OLTP database that faces customers. Replacing this structure with a fact-dimensional structure as shown in Figure 6.2 shows the schemas in Figure 6.4 and Figure 6.6, reducing both the number of tables and the complexity of the relationships between those tables; reducing the number tables is critical to SQL query join performance. Data warehouses consist of large quantities of data, batch updates, and sometimes incredibly complex analytical queries; this makes fewer tables in joins even more important. The piece of code following is a SQL join query joining all nine tables in the snowflake schema as shown in Figure 6.5. If the SALE fact table has 1 million rows and all dimensions contain 10 rows each, then a Cartesian product would return 10^6 multiplied by 10^9 $(10^1 + 10^1 + 10^1 + \ldots + \ldots$, or nine times, or 10^9) rows. That would be a result of 10^{15} rows $(10^9 \times 10^6 = 10^{15})$, and that is a huge amount of data for current computing technology to process.

A Cartesian product is a worst-case scenario, but I am trying to make the point in the extreme of the increased amount of data retrieved with the more tables involved in a join, without going into the nitty-gritty details of how the various joins should or should not be performed.

```
SELECT * FROM SALE JOIN AUTHOR
        JOIN CUSTOMER
                JOIN SUPPLIER
                        JOIN SUBJECT
                                JOIN CATEGORY
                                        JOIN BOOK
                                                JOIN PUBLISHER
                                                        JOIN
PUBLICATION
WHERE ...
GROUP BY ...
ORDER BY ... ;
```

Now look at the next query, which uses the star schema shown in Figure 6.7, and assuming the same number of rows, a join occurs between one fact table and six dimensional tables. The result is a Cartesian product of 10^6 multiplied by 10^6, which yields a resulting 10^{12} rows returned. The difference between 10^{12} and 10^{15} is three decimals, and three decimals is not just three zeroes (1,000 rows) but is 1,000,000,000,000,000 − 1,000,000,000,000 = 999,000,000,000,000, which is just a little shy of 10^{15}. And so the difference between six dimensions and nine dimensions (a reduction of three tables in the join) is more or less infinite from the perspective of counting all those zeroes. Therefore, fewer dimensions definitely makes for much faster queries, because it can drastically reduce the quantity of data you have to read, which is why it is so essential to denormalize snowflake schemas into star schemas.

```
SELECT * FROM SALE JOIN AUTHOR
        JOIN CUSTOMER
                JOIN SUPPLIER
                        JOIN SUBJECT
                                JOIN BOOK
WHERE ...
GROUP BY ...
ORDER BY ... ;
```

- Take another quick glance at the snowflake schema in Figure 6.4 and Figure 6.5, and then examine the equivalent denormalized star schema in Figure 6.6 and Figure 6.7. Now put yourself into the shoes of a hustled, harried, and very busy executive trying to get a quick report and only being interested in results. Which diagram is easier to decipher as to content and meaning? The diagram in Figure 6.7 or the more complex diagram in Figure 6.5? After all, being an end user, you are probably not too interested in understanding the complexities of how to build SQL join queries, as you probably have bigger fish to fry. The point is that the less complex the table structure, the easier it will be to use, because a star schema is more representative of the real world than a snowflake schema. Look at it this way: a snowflake schema is more deeply normalized than a star schema and therefore by definition more mathematical. Something more mathematical is generally of more use to a mathematician than it is to an executive manager, where the executive is trying to get a quick overall impression of whether his company will sell more cans of lima beans or more cans of string beans over the course of the next 10 years. The driving force behind database modeling should be the desired result—you have to see the bigger picture in some respects without getting too bogged down in the details.

6.2.3 Kimball and Inmon on Data Warehousing

A lot of people contributed to the creation of the data warehouse model, all the way back to the 1960s. The most well-known contributors are Ralph Kimball (www.kimballgroup.com) and Bill Inmon (www.inmon.com). Kimball put forward the fact dimensional, star, and snowflake schema data warehouse model. Inmon subsequently added to the data warehouse model by allowing data warehouses to be a 3rd normal form normalized architecture. The modern data warehouse model fits Inmon's expansion best, where a typical data warehouse consists of a 3rd normal form staging database in addition to a fact-dimensional data warehouse; Kimball's ideas do not include any kind of staging environment. Kimball also broke the fact-dimensional structure into multiple data marts, where each data mart is a fact table that can be connected with a bus structure containing common

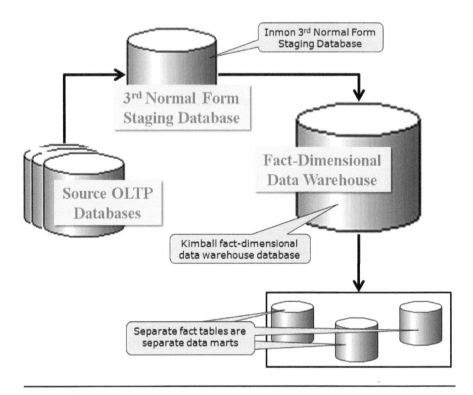

Figure 6.8   Modern data warehouse 3rd normal form architecture.

elements across data marts. Figure 6.8 shows the basic architecture of a typical modern data warehouse including data marts, which break up transactional data into multiple fact tables.

This section has described the very basics of data warehouse database modeling. How can a data warehouse database model be constructed?

6.2.3.1 Slowly Changing Dimensions (Types)

In some applications, such as the medical industry, it is necessary to retain a history of static dimensional data changes—for example, so that multiple historical versions of the same customer's information can be retained. Obviously, the appropriate version of a customer would be connected to the correct facts in any related fact tables, which due to their historical nature already retain archived data. The result is that because dimensions are relatively static in comparison to facts, then multiple versions of the same dimension are still relatively static when compared to facts, and thus they are known as *slowly changing dimensions* (as opposed to *static dimensions*). There are seven types of slowly changing dimensions ranging in complexity from the basic to the more complex, named as *Type 0* through *Type 6*. The different type definitions store different types and amounts of information used to denote the difference between multiple versions of the same data and how dimensions are related to facts. Slowly changing dimensions are not complicated but should be mentioned as they are important in some applications where meticulous historical records must be kept when compared to facts.

> Many data warehouses do not retain enough detail in fact tables to make it necessary to retain multiple versions of the same dimensions, to facilitate relating multiple versioned dimensions to facts at different periods of times. This is especially the case where facts are summarized and become grouped numerical values, where data such as customer dimensions can begin to become meaningless. What is needed depends on the environment and the reporting requirements.

6.3 Data Warehouse Modeling

Now you know how to build star schemas for data warehouse database models, and as you can see, a star schema is quite different from a standard relational database model like that shown in Figure 6.1. The next step is to examine the process and the steps by which a data warehouse database model can be built.

The primary objective of a data warehouse—of any database for that matter—is to service end users. The end users are the people who read reports produced by data warehouse SQL queries and utilize a data warehouse to search for patterns, attempting to forecast trends from large amounts of historical information. So it follows that there must be a sequence of steps in approaching data warehouse database design, which begins with the end-user perspective and the business processes of a company:

- **Business Processes.** Establish the subject areas of a business as, in how a business can be divided up. The answer is the fact tables, where fact tables (data marts) contain a detailed history of transactions.
- **Granularity.** Granularity is the level of detail required and should be thought about and discussed before beginning to build a data warehouse, especially before you start building ETL (Extract Transport and Load) code and pushing data into your new data warehouse database. There are three facets to granularity: (1) the number of table columns added to fact tables, (2) the level of row detail to be added and maintained, and (3) how far back into the past your data should record (how old must data be before you can delete it).
- **Identify and Build Dimensions.** Dimensions contain static information that describes facts and must be built before facts, because facts contain foreign key references back to dimension tables. Dimensions can also contain multiple versions if necessary.
- **Build Facts.** Once again, facts are transactional records that can go back many years.

6.3.1 Understanding Business Processes

This step is analytical in nature but crucial, as it really helps you as a data modeler to understand what the needs of the business are, as much as they can be assessed beforehand. In some respects, much of this type of analytical work will involve analyzing existing OLTP normalized databases to figure out where the data will come from. When it comes to who is going to use the data warehouse, reviewing any existing reporting architecture is probably going to be a lot of help.

6.3.2 Granularity

As already stated, granularity is the level of detail required, which consists of three facets: (1) the number of columns added to fact tables, (2) the depth of row detail to be added, and (3) how much historical data is to be retained. Firstly, if you add too few columns and row details (only currently known to be required), you may have to update your data warehouse in the future when new requirements are requested. Updating existing fact tables in a data warehouse with more data in the future may not be a problem if your data warehouse is small and you have some really expensive hardware. However, if you get into database sizes of multiple terabytes or larger, and you try to update fact tables and you have poor I/O capacity, and the end-user population is using the data—you could have a difficult performance problem. On the contrary, a smaller data warehouse may be easy to update as new requirements arise. In truth, what you should do is to assess the environment and what is needed first before diving in.

The trouble with storing every single transaction and every column from every source database table is that your data warehouse fact tables will probably get very big very quickly, and you probably will not need data like strings if they are not described by dimensions, as well as converted to dimensions. If you simply do not know what data will be required, then the most prudent approach might be to include all historical data down to the lowest level of granularity. This ensures that any data needed in the future will not be missing. The downside to keeping everything possible is that your database will get big; on the contrary, not including all detail might leave you with updates that could well be too time consuming to absorb. There are specialized objects such as materialized views that can create summaries at a later stage on top of detailed data, which can help to speed up reading of data from the data warehouse—but your data warehouse is still going to get big.

6.3.2.1 How Long to Retain Data Warehouse Data

The amount of time you keep data in a data warehouse depends on end-user requirements, but generally when data is no longer useful it can be removed on a temporal basis. So it is important that when seeking to somehow divide up or partition a data warehouse fact table, you should seriously consider dividing up data by some kind of date, such as a full time stamp, months, quarters, or years; if you do not, then in the future when your data warehouse is really huge, the removal of out-of-date and unneeded data could cripple performance for your data warehouse—perhaps even for days at a time. Some data warehouses retain all data forever, but when a data warehouse becomes too difficult to manage, there will have to be some deletion or summarizing of older data, or both.

> Be warned! Summarizing data warehouse records into aggregated records, and deleting detail records can be a seriously time-consuming effort if done when a data warehouse is large.

It all depends on hardware storage capacity, the power of the computers at hand, and how much you can spend on continually expanding the capacity of existing hardware. Upgrading a large data warehouse to new hardware and software can also be very time consuming if you have to copy from one storage medium to another.

6.3.3 Commonly Occurring Types of Dimension Tables

The data warehouse database models for the REVIEW and SALE database models as shown previously in this chapter are not the best they could be. Many data warehouse databases have standard requirements based on how end users need to analyze data, and there are thus some commonly used additional dimensions such as dates, locations, and product categories. These additional dimensions can be built from most types of transactional data by parsing through transactions as they are loaded into the data warehouse, giving much better scope and usefulness to the data in a data warehouse.

Invoicing or any type of transactions involving invoicing and payments on products or services are usually dated, and therefore every transaction can be placed (or dated) into a specific period. Locations can usually be assessed from customers, suppliers, shippers, and other companies that there is contact with. The REVIEW and SALE fact tables shown in Figure 6.2 and Figure 6.6 both contain date columns (REVIEW.REVIEW_DATE and SALE.SALE_DATE), and a resulting date or timestamp dimension might look something like that shown in Figure 6.9, where temporal information is summarized by month, quarter, and year; temporal information can be

Time

time_id
month
quarter
year

Figure 6.9   A time dimension entity.

more detailed, but that can become cumbersome, and the business may never need that level of that detail. Date columns in the tables would be replaced with identifiers, as shown in Figure 6.10.

Figure 6.10 shows fact tables for both book reviews and sales, where the date columns have been replaced with foreign key links to the TIME table. The result of this is that facts can be analyzed by month, quarter, and year. Removing the date columns from the fact tables has decreased the level of detail required—unless, of course, you will want to analyze your data in future by week, day, hour, minute, second, and so on.

> You do not have to remove date and timestamp columns from the fact tables, but the result is that temporal values cannot be summarized numerically.

Another commonly used dimension involves locations, where demographic identifiers such as states, cities, countries, continents, and regions can be extracted and connected to facts. Location details for review and sale facts can be extracted from customer and shipper address details in reviews and sales, respectively. The resulting LOCATION table could look something like that shown in Figure 6.11; some silly columns have been added just to give this conversation a little color, and the equivalent star schema changes are shown in Figure 6.12 (on page 190).

There are many other possible types of dimensions that are common to many data warehouses, which can cover topic areas such as products and product categories, error tracking dimensions to measure the quality of data, as well as junk, degenerate, or even role-playing dimensions.

> A junk dimension is an abstraction containing items with low cardinality such as multiple Y/N fields. Degenerate dimensions contain values directly related to the primary key of the fact table, such as a shipping bill of lading number or an invoice number. A role-playing dimension is something like a date that can be used in more ways than one, such as representing different date types for the same date in time.

The form and types of additional dimensions depend on the data content of a data warehouse and how the data warehouse is to be used. Again,

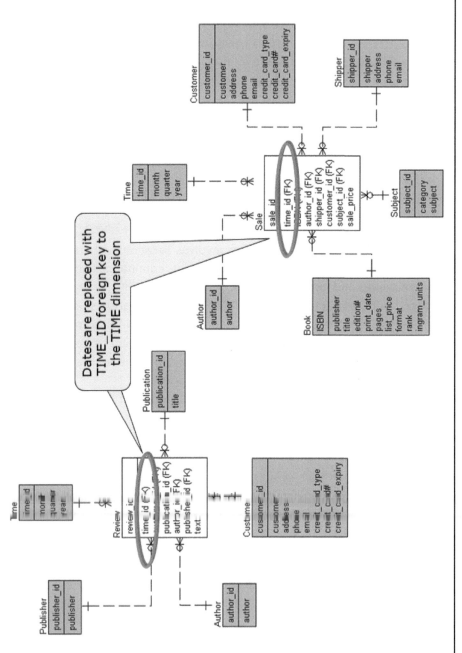

Figure 6.10 Adding the time dimension to the facts.

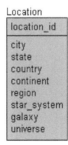

Figure 6.11   Location dimensions are commonly used to analyze data by region.

a word of caution: adding new dimensions after the fact could involve huge amounts of I/O as changes to fact tables would be required, especially in the case where your fact tables are extremely large.

6.3.4 Understanding the Basics of Fact Tables

Fact tables generally contain three types of columns: (1) foreign keys pointing to dimensions, (2) numerical values that can be summarized, and (3) non-numeric values that cannot be summarized.

> The non-numeric values could take up too much space and cause performance problems in future, so be cautious about including them. However, not including them means that data is lost. Can you answer the question that those non-numerical columns will not be required in the future? Or can they be added in the future if they are requested by users?

Foreign keys in fact tables that point to dimensions are not facts and are often surrogate keys unique to the fact table (not always originating in a source OLTP database), meaning their values are generated when the fact tables are loaded. Fact tables can contain detailed transactional histories, summaries (aggregations), or both. Details and aggregations can be separated into different fact tables, and many relational databases allow use of materialized views to contain fact table aggregations; materialized views store less detailed aggregations of their originating fact tables.

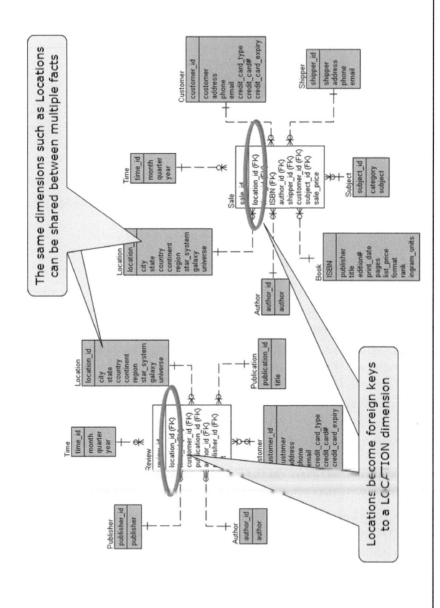

Figure 6.12 Adding a location dimension to facts.

One of the most significant factors with fact tables, specifically because of their potentially enormous size, is how fact tables are changed. Fact tables can be added to or changed and even deleted from. The least obstructive change (least resource intensive) to a fact table is adding new data, and more specifically, only ever appending data (adding to the end of), and also preferably during low end-user activity time windows. Deletion from fact tables may be necessary when upgrading to more summarized details or perhaps mass deletion of old data that is no longer useful. Fact tables are thus regarded as being additive, semi-additive, or non-additive. The most efficient data warehouses are those that never change and contain only non-additive fact tables.

Every data warehouse is different and depends largely on requirements, as well as the data modeler and ETL programmers having as much information as possible about to the future needs of the data warehouse. You can create a data warehouse generically, but it is risky because the less insider company knowledge the builders have, the more generic and abstract their approach has to be. So in any data warehouse project, always include someone who knows a lot about the business of the company, and make sure that the insider is high enough up the management scale to have the power to request items such as more computing power and resources, otherwise your data warehouse project may hobble along on one leg in perpetuity. A data warehouse can be unexpectedly expensive to both build and maintain, and management needs to know just how big, complicated, and expensive a large data warehouse project can become.

Figure 6.13 shows the tables of a database containing the details of bands, their released CDs, and tracks on each of those CDs. There are also three tables containing royalty amounts earned by each track from radio plays, live performances, and recordings by other artists. Firstly, create an equivalent data warehouse snowflake schema, and secondly, denormalize the snowflake schema into a more efficient star schema.

1. Identify the fact tables. Facts are generally business processes of the day-to-day functions of a business. Transactional data is functional.
2. Granularity can be ignored in this case.
3. What are the dimensions? Dimensions are the static tables in a data warehouse database model.
4. Create the dimension tables followed by the fact tables.

To find the solution and build a fact table, let's go through the process in steps as follows:

1. In Figure 6.13 the transactional tables contain constantly changing royalties (the ROYALTY_AMOUNT columns). The royalty tables are the RADIO, PERFORMANCE, and RECORDING tables, and these three tables are the only tables with royalty amount and date values in them, which makes them transactional tables (fact tables).
2. In Figure 6.13 the dimensions are all the tables containing static data, which are the BAND, CD, and TRACK tables.
3. The next step is to begin by building dimension tables and then building fact tables after that. Figure 6.14 shows a simplistic picture of all static dimensions and facts in the form of a dimensionally normalized snowflake schema.

   Figure 6.15 shows the ERD equivalent of the snowflake schema shown in Figure 6.14. Note how date and location values are replaced

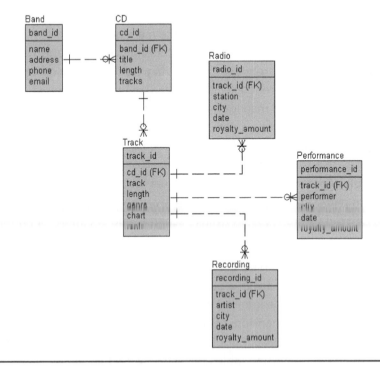

Figure 6.13   An OLTP relational database model.

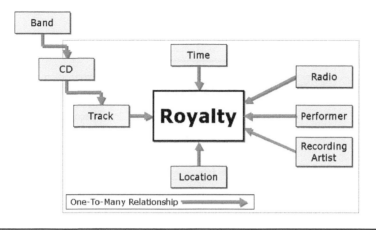

Figure 6.14   A data warehouse snowflake schema.

by dimensions TIME and LOCATION (shown both in Figure 6.14 and Figure 6.15).

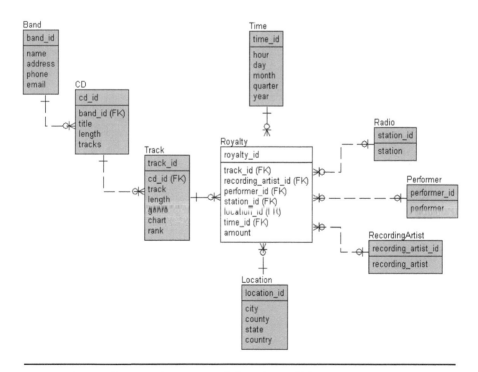

Figure 6.15   A data warehouse snowflake schema ERD.

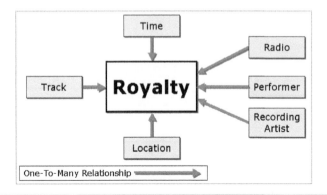

Figure 6.16   A data warehouse star schema.

4. Figure 6.16 and Figure 6.17 show a conversion of a snowflake to star schema where the BAND, CD, and TRACK tables are all denormalized into the single dimension table called TRACK—the result is a single-level hierarchy of dimensions.

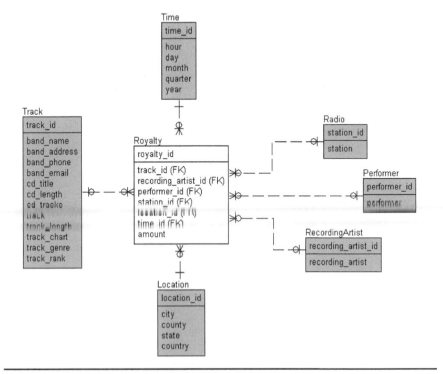

Figure 6.17   A data warehouse star schema ERD.

6.4 Conclusion

This chapter covered:

- The origin of data warehouses and why a transactional (OLTP) database model is often inadequate for internal analysis and reporting.
- Data warehouses can require specialized database modeling techniques in the form of facts and dimensions.
- Star schemas are a single dimensional layer and can provide the best efficiency and clarity to end-users.
- Snowflake schemas are normalized and less efficient forms of star schemas because they increase join sizes on very large tables.
- Facts contain variable data, which are the history of a company's transactional activities.
- Dimensions contain static data that describes facts.
- Dimensions describe the facts by normalizing only static (dimensional) data, preferably in a single dimensional layer a star and not a snowflake schema.
- Fact-dimensional database modeling is either a star schema or a snowflake schema.
- Data warehouses can contain one or more fact tables, which are linked to the same shared dimensions or a subset of those dimensions.
- The steps and processes in building a data warehouse database model.
- The contents of a data warehouse database and model.

This chapter has described the specialized database modeling techniques that may be required for building data warehouses. The next chapter will examine specialized data warehouse modeling as well as BigData modeling.

Chapter 7

Modeling for BigData Databases

Big data is at the foundation of all of the megatrends that are happening today, from social to mobile to the cloud, to gaming.[*]

—Chris Lynch

Less can be so much more.

The previous chapter dug deeply into the details of the database warehouse database model, including the different types of schemas, components, and how they fit together. This chapter expands into some of the most recently prominent data modeling techniques in the realm of data warehouse staging and BigData. Even though the field of BigData is a very large topic, from the data modeling perspective, in BigData the modeling is much less about metadata and schemas and logical structure—it is more about the combination of the architecture of both logical and physical structures that comprise an entire ecosystem of hardware and software making up a BigData framework.

This chapter covers:

---

* https://www.weforum.org/agenda/2015/01/the-most-revealing-big-data-quotes/

- Staging databases for data warehouses and BigData databases
- Defining BigData modeling
- Different types of BigData models
- Columnar Database Modeling
- Key-Value Store Modeling
- Document Collection Data Modeling
- Graph Data Modeling

7.1 Dimensional Modeling and Staging Databases in the Age of BigData

Inmon's form of the data warehouse model is subject oriented and applies across an entire enterprise using a normalized table structure. Modern warehouses and BigData databases can often be augmented with a specialized 3rd normal form relational staging database (see Figure 7.1, repeated from Figure 6.8).

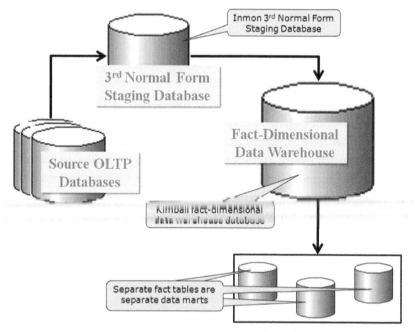

Figure 7.1   Modern data warehouse 3rd normal form staging plus warehouse architecture, repeated from Figure 6.8.

A staging database is often used to pre-build warehouse objects in a pre-constructed (staged) database, in order to remove the warehouse small-scale precision database changes from the warehouse, such as incremental changes (UPDATE and DELETE commands). Incremental changes are small scale and not warehouse friendly, and small-scale changes can perform much better in a 3rd normal form data model that allows indexing (the most efficient data warehouse models do not have any indexes). A staging database is used as an alternative to moving directly from relational database to warehouse, which can cause huge performance problems in modern custom-built warehouses because there are no indexes. Note that joins between relational tables that apply filtering require indexing in order to avoid reading all rows in all tables, which can make for very inefficient filtered joins, because, for example, a filter that expects to read 1% of a large table will read the entire table when no indexing is available.

Temporal data is difficult to manage without a specialized normalized staging database, because often the only way to work effectively with data that has been generated over time is to work with it by reading it in date order. Otherwise, the result is often to have to constantly reorganize and copy that temporal data into functional structures and sorted orders so that consumers of the data can work with the data by function. Kimball's straightforward fact-dimensional model is that it over-generalizes requirements by generating a quick functional-based solution, which is implemented in a way that is easily interpreted and often appreciated by functional business users linking separate fact-dimensional star schemas (data marts). So Kimball's model can be better suited to functionally organized, as opposed to temporally sorted, data.

Following on from Figure 7.1 and the 3rd normal form staging database model, there are some specific 3rd normal form data models that apply to data warehousing that have specific purposes, in the form of the data vault model and the anchor model.

7.1.1 The Data Vault Model

The data vault model is useful for working with a history of data change, which allows for tracking of where change originates from when there are multiple sources of data. The data vault model also includes a temporal history of when and as changes occurred. The data vault model is not used to store completely cleansed data in that it can contain data not conforming to business rules. With these structural limits, the data vault model can be useful for scalable, very high parallel processed insert only performance, where past events can be tracked and replayed, but not with 100% accuracy (un-cleansed data can contain errors that are permitted in favor of speed). Figure 7.2 shows a copy of a simple data warehouse star schema from Figure 6.6, and Figure 7.3 shows an equivalent data vault model form of the same schema from Figure 7.2.

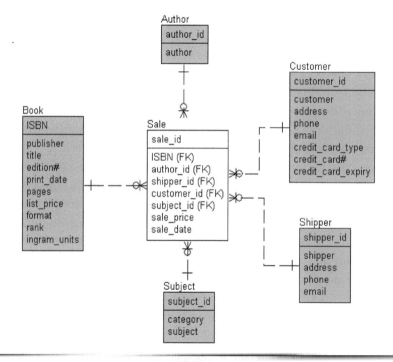

Figure 7.2   A simple star schema for books and customers, repeated from Figure 6.6

The data vault model is a form of 3rd normal form star schema structure, where entity types consist of the following:

- **Hub.** Hubs contain infrequently changed business key functions, showing the HUB_BOOK and HUB_CUSTOMER entities in Figure 7.3 (shown as *Hub_<tablename>* in Figure 7.3). Hubs are indexed with a surrogate primary key and a non-surrogate business key. The business key uniquely represents each item in the business function, such

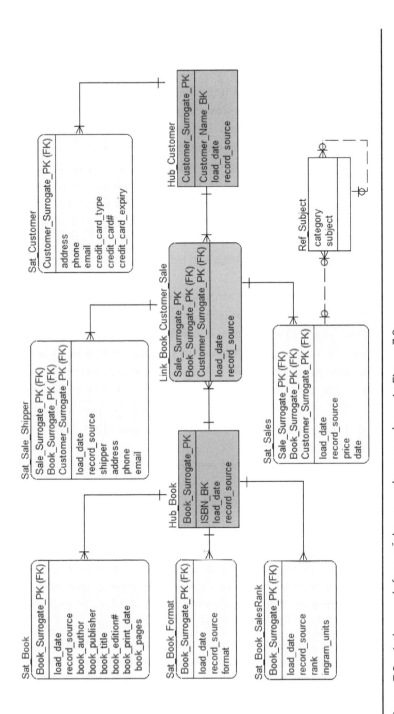

Figure 7.3 A data vault form of the star schema as shown in Figure 7.2.

as an ISBN (International Standard Book Number) to uniquely represent a book. Note that hubs contain only keys plus a record of where data was sourced, as well as when the data was added; hubs do not contain data attributes that describe the data, such as a customer's address and phone number describing the customer.

- **Link.** Links form transactions between two business functions as associative entities (many-to-many join resolution entities), such as the sale of a book to a customer or LINK_BOOK_CUSTOMER_SALE (shown as *Link_<tablename>* in Figure 7.3). Similar to a hub, a link contains only keys, plus the source of data and when that data was loaded. Links can link to other links, but that is poor practice because it can cause problems with high-speed parallel insert processing, as a result of duplication of link keys and potential sharing of satellite entities (see Satellite, below).

- **Satellite.** Satellites are the only entities containing data attributes (actual data), or in technical jargon non-metadata items that do not consist of keys or loading data (where data originated and when it was loaded). Thus Satellites contain data such as when a book was sold and for how much in the SAT_SALES table (shown *Sat_<tablename>* in Figure 7.3). So hubs and links form data model structure or metadata, and satellites contain descriptive data that preferably groups data into different satellites depending on how often the non-metadata values are updated.

- **Reference.** Reference entities are extra-structural entities that contain non-keyed and non-key referenced static data items that are referred to in satellite entities only.

So the purpose of the data vault model is for very high-speed rapid parallel data insertion only, where reads can help to audit and track both the source of data, as well as where each data value originates, as well as the date of the insertion. The data vault model is generally not used by business users because it is normalized and thus will appear complex and cryptic to those other than technical people but can serve well as source for other connected business-facing data sources and applications.

Data warehouse and BigData processing often source very large amounts of data across heterogeneous environments, including multifarious database vendors and sources, such as Oracle, SQL Server, IoT, even other warehouses and perhaps even flat or Microsoft Excel files, possibly even online feeds. The world of warehouses and particularly BigData can be complex and originate copious amounts of hard-to-sift-through data, and from many sources all at the same time. A data vault model can be useful to help pre-construct and stage some or all of the huge amounts of data being constantly pushed into modern data warehouse and BigData environments.

7.1.2 The Anchor Model

The data vault model creates 3rd normal form table structures, which would not be appropriate for modern data warehouses that lack indexes, such as Netezza®, Vertica®, Snowflake®, and Redshift. What this means ultimately is that building a normalized data model inside a non-relational data warehouse will likely result in huge performance problems when trying to change and join data using indexes, where those indexes either are not catered to or they exist but are not active and are only present for modeling purposes. Data warehouses like the ones mentioned above get their speed by full scanning tables en masse using partition pruning to remove unwanted data, as well as executing against multiple partitions in parallel.

This discussion leads to the agile anchor data model, used in both warehouses and OLTP databases, which can be normalized as far as 6th normal form. The anchor model may apply most sensibly when building a warehouse on a relational platform such as Oracle® or Postgres, but it is unlikely to be useful in a modern data warehouse platform. Modern data warehouses divide up data and processing using physical distribution of data with horizontal (distribution by row) and vertical (distribution by column) purtitlonlng, sometimes culled sharding.

> Sharding is often confused with horizontal or vertical partitioning, or even both. Sharding is very similar to partitioning but also adds in the aspect of distributing separate shards (partitions) across separate server instances (metal or virtual). The overall effect is separated clusters of data in a clustered or grid-like architecture of many machines, which may not necessarily be required to be up to date with each other.

So the anchor model normalizes the data vault even further with the result of creating a model that is almost plug and play scalable, where changes are added and not modified, but can lead to hugely detailed and complex models. The anchor model consists of the following structures:

- **Anchor**. Business entities like data vault hubs and have primary keys only.
- **Attributes**. More highly normalized data vault satellites where an attribute contains the descriptive attributes of a single anchor only.
- **Ties**. Similar to data vault links creating a relationship between the anchor business entities but allowing for easier modification than the data vault model.
- **Knots**. These are attributes that are shared between two or more anchor business entities such as low cardinality static data entities; for example, country names or categories.

> Attributes can be temporally enabled to create archive-capable structure as with hubs, links, and satellites in the data vault model.

One of the problems with the data vault model, and more so the anchor model, is that even though normalization helps with precision and accuracy, it can lead to performance problems in both relational and modern architected data warehouses, and even in relational databases because of its level of detail. Normalized data warehouse models are presented in this chapter because they are still an option for smaller data sets, and with very specific applications.

7.1.3 Connecting the Dots from Relations and Dimensions Through to BigData

Database modeling has been around for a long time, including the relational normalized and warehouse fact-dimensional models. In addition, object database models allow the embedding of objects where relational database vendors such as Oracle and Microsoft® were quick to rise to the occasion and attempt to compete with object databases by embedding externally interpretable code (XML and JSON), and allowing binary objects to be included inline with rows in relational tables.

The result was the object-relational database model that culminated in interpretable XML and JSON type structures that can be embedded into relational database tables and interpreted with custom APIs (Application Programming Interface), which is essentially embedding data and data semantics (metadata) into relational databases, creating NoSQL data objects inside relational databases.

The problem with the larger relational database vendors is that the products that won the biggest market shares increased their prices to such exorbitant levels that open source databases eventually appeared for two reasons: (1) the cost of a database like Oracle was exorbitant, and (2) databases like Oracle tried to do everything and specialized open source databases did better at specific tasks (specific business use case). The success of modern and open source databases resulted in more specialized environments that targeted narrower areas of application in order to compete with companies such as Oracle.

So now Oracle Corporation is buying up application software because of the new database competition and transforming itself into an applications vendor rather than a database vendor—even buying up and expanding upon open source products such as MySQL.

> It is a common misconception that open source software is free, which it is not because it is often supported for a fee, as well as having an open development process that anyone can contribute to, including end users. The meaning of open source is that the source code is accessible and can be changed and improved upon (or forked into something else), both collaboratively and collectively.

Filling in the gaps of functionality with new ideas are new inventions like NoSQL databases, such as the document collection MongoDB® database, which is structured as containers within containers and embedded NoSQL schema-less functionality executing the contents of JSON files. There are also simplistic key-value stores that are completely flexible, and even graph databases that are used to represent the complexity of nodes connecting to any other node across a complex network of nodes. So the next step is to proceed on to BigData modeling.

7.2 What Is BigData Modeling?

Compared to traditional relational data modeling, BigData is less complex but also has less substance to it with respect to drawing entity relationship diagrams. BigData modeling is more about the flow of data and all the elements in an entire ecosystem that both uses and surrounds the data. BigData modeling is about designing an entire ecosystem rather than just a schema or schematic blueprint of what data should look like. This is because BigData databases are built as a system encompassing all the elements in that system, as opposed to in a database engine. In reality, there is not much in a BigData ecosystem that is new and has not been thought of already in the past, except that BigData is just very much bigger, and that all the pieces of the data puzzle are better linked together and put together in one place.

BigData models are very simplistic from the entity perspective in that they tend to flatten tables even more than a data warehouse, such as in the completely denormalized transition shown in Figure 7.4. Figure 7.4 shows separate flattened-out business functions that are similar to flattened data warehouse star schemas connected by many-to-many datamart bus joins.

Figure 7.5 shows a very high-level physical system model structure for a simple sample BigData environment ecosystem containing all the different parts in a data-centric application workflow.

7.2.1 Some Useful BigData Modeling Terminology

There are some interesting terms that have appeared or been more frequently utilized since the advent of BigData and are useful to discuss briefly:

- **Data Store**. A storage medium for data without metadata stored with it, storing data in a schema-less manner.
- **Analytics**. The process of analyzing data to attempt to discover new insights.
- **Data Science**. Many disciplines including statistics, mathematics, computer science, communication and business knowledge—all used to extract insights and knowledge from data (similar to analytics).
- **Data Governance**. An enterprise-wide approach applying a set of rules with a governing body that is used for managing data as a whole. These rules include the following: data availability, data accessibility,

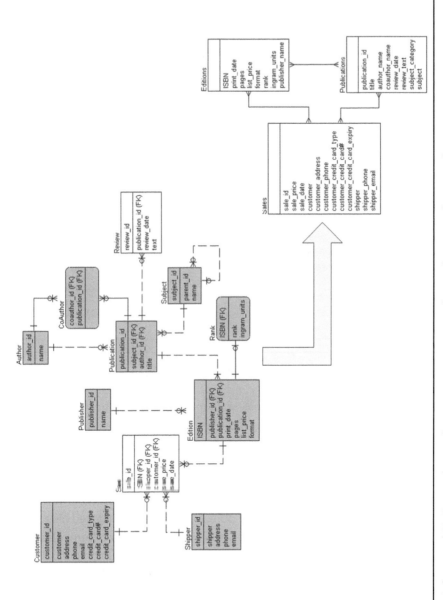

Figure 7.4 A flattened BigData schema showing separate equivalents of separate business functions.

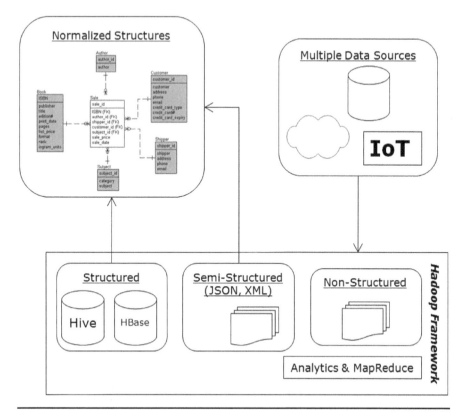

Figure 7.5   A simple sample BigData model ecosystem.

data usability, data cleanliness, data makes sense, data integrity (error free), data security including policies or rules used to apply security and match to SLAs (Service Level Agreements) in order to set expectations with clientele.

- **Data Lake.** A data lake is a broad concept that allows storage of everything across an entire organization, which can include unformatted data in the form of embedded binary objects, externally structured data such as XML, JSON, Excel, or CSV files, and even data sourced from relational databases. A data lake allows access from a high-level conceptual perspective, enterprise wide across a company, effectively linking together machine learning plus analytical processing, connecting to a large and flexible data source that is constantly changing as data within it changes. A data swamp is another form of a data lake, but is a deteriorated and unmanaged data lake that provides little value to users.

- **Flexible Datatypes and Unstructured Data**. These datatypes are object datatypes, possibly stored in binary format, used to store data in a database that might have semantics to the data, but the semantics does not extend any meaning outside of the object. This is the type of datatype where schema-less embedded objects such as JSON or XML documents would be stored. Binary and text objects have been embedded in object and relational databases for decades and are extensively used in BigData data stores to encode and transparently store embedded schema-less data, such as JSON objects.

- **Landing and Flattened Tables**. Landing tables are often the first table where post ETL (Extract Transport and Load) processing data is moved from a data source such as MongoDB. Flattened tables usually refer to joined tables and will likely be in various stages of denormalization. Landing and flattened tables can include joined tables as well as removal of embedded data semantics that were stored in datatypes containing JSON or XML.

- **Predictive Modeling**. Models become more accurate with more data, and data quantities and variable options are growing ever larger all the time. BigData provides a lot of data and, statistically, the larger a sample size becomes then the more accurate the results get.

- **Visualization.** Tools such as Tableau®, Qlik®, and Looker® are used to rapidly create visually appealing, easily understandable, and user- or business-friendly pictures of data.

- **Recommendation Engine.** This is a tool that is used to match a customer with the next choice of item they might purchase online, and then target that person with the appropriate online marketing.

- **Machine Learning.** A subset of AI (Artificial Intelligence) that utilizes algorithms, statistical modeling, and computers to infer results and patterns in data without all the facts, thus inference or an educated guess.

- **Python and R.** Python can be used to write programs with very large unstructured BigData datasets. R is a more complex and specialized language and is more appropriate for structured datasets.

7.2.2 *Comparing ACID and BASE Consistency Models*

ACID implies that once a transaction is complete, its data is consistent; this is also called *write consistency*. ACID stands for the following:

- **Atomic**. All operations in a transaction will succeed completely or be rolled back (undone) completely.
- **Consistent**. The database has structural integrity once the transaction is complete.
- **Isolated**. There is no contention between transactions, meaning that multiple transactions do not operate on the same data at the same time, by way of automated multi-transactional locks that force what is effectively sequential processing by executing separate successive transactions one after the other, without interfering with each other, on the same row in a table.
- **Durable**. Transactions apply change permanently.

Databases that require precision and accurate data integrity use the ACID model, such as all relational databases and some other databases, including graph database engines. ACID transactions are pessimistic and do not allow for any data integrity errors, whereas the BASE model can allow for some error. Modern data warehouse and BigData databases are so large that disk read and write throughput is far more important than 100% data integrity, and thus data warehouses built inside relational databases can be more efficient when no referential integrity is applied. In fact, data warehouse databases can allow a measurable amount of error in data, and thus it follows that BigData databases have loosened requirements for data consistency between separate copies, including data not having to be up to date throughout a data store, and data does not have to be 100% accurate. Modern data warehouses and more so BigData databases are designed with better scale and resilience of data, as opposed to requiring 100% accuracy and integrity. They use the BASE model:

- **Basic Availability**. A database is only expected to work most of the time.
- **Soft State**. Write consistency of data is not required, and multiple mirrored copies of that data do not have to be all the same at all times.
- **Eventual Consistency**. Data sets are assumed to eventually be consistent with each other but are not required to be immediately.

The HBASE database is an example of a BASE modeled database engine, which is a column-based (column-partitioned) database management system that executes on top of the Hadoop framework HDFS (Hadoop Distributed File System) data storage tool.

Why is it significant to compare the ACID and the BASE models? This is because the transition from relational database model, to data warehouse database model, and finally to BigData database model has been a step-by-step process that has gradually substituted data integrity and precision for processing speed of larger and larger quantities of data; data warehouses and BigData databases are most significantly affected by disk speed throughput.

Database modeling has simplified over time, as it has had to adapt to huge volumes of data that could always benefit from the accuracy of the ACID model, but the huge quantities would slow down larger warehouse and BigData databases to a point where a data lake might turn into an unusable data swamp.

Also where ACID databases track and utilize transactional change, warehouses and BigData databases predict trends over large samples of data over time. Going further, BigData databases search for unknown patterns in huge volumes of data, where accuracy improves as sample sizes increase, and thus the need for 100% accuracy and integrity becomes statistically unnecessary as growing data sample sizes increase the accuracy of results.

7.2.3 Risks with BigData Modeling

The risk with BigData is that fast ingestion of data encourages scale and volume, and just as when constantly appended to data warehouses, a Big-Data database gets bigger and bigger until much of what is stored can become a data swamp (a deteriorated data lake) and not useful.

The lack of a data model inside a BigData ecosystem such as a data lake is useful for flexibility, but it can help to explain why data scientists working with the large data sources tend to spend, and perhaps waste, at least 80% of their valuable time cleaning and organizing data; this leaves a mere 20% of their time doing real data science and creative discovery work.

Isolating some of the more important parts of a BigData database inside a very large ecosystem can help to speed up analytics and engineering of results, simply because when searching for results, one needs to read what is most relevant. For example, geographical and demographic data is often very important for BigData setups where analytical and visualization products such as Tableau and Qlik are used, which can provide very rapid and user-friendly insight into the meaning of data without having to understand the internal structure and intra-relationships within that data. So flattening absolutely everything may not always be the most sensible option.

7.2.4 Schema on Read (Schema-Less)

Schema-less implies that a BigData data store does not attach metadata into the database itself, even though embedding JSON objects does embed data semantics into the data. Not imposing a model on data increases loading and writing performance when ingesting data into a data store, but read performance can as a result be adversely affected by having to apply an interpretable structure (a schema) as data is read from a data store. The result is the following:

- Initial loading is very fast.
- Data stores get overly large because of lack of attention paid to insertions, as a result of rapid insertion speed.
- Subsequent changes to existing data are somewhere between extremely slow and perhaps even impossible.
- Subsequent reads apply a schematic as data is read and can be very slow.

7.2.4.1 SQL vs. NoSQL (Not-SQL or Schema-Less)

NoSQL is a dynamic structure that can be easily changed because there is an implied rather than applied structure. On the contrary, a SQL schema'd database is static because it has static metadata objects stored inside the data store for things such as tables and columns. So the relational model is static because it is predefined, and NoSQL is not static because it is not predefined as part of database functionality and is much more flexible as a result. NoSQL objects use flexibly defined metadata stored in JSON objects rather than embedded into the database like a relational database does.

Modern databases are going back in time to the days before the relational database and becoming more specialized, in that a database vendor engine, such as MongoDB or Redshift, has a much more specific function or use case than a relational database like Oracle does. Pre-relational database engines were much the same, in that they were specialized, but they were specialized because database modeling was an underdeveloped science. So it follows that, in the modern era of open-source databases and frustration with the cost of products like Oracle that attempt everything, the result is many different products with many different functional use cases. Modern databases such as MongoDB, HBASE®, and Vertica have very specialized functions that a database engine like Oracle attempted to do all in the same database engine, with mixed results. One of the primary reasons for many new database engines is a need for extreme performance in specific use cases. Some of the more modern databases are shown in Figure 7.6, including many post-relational era specialized object-like open source and cloud database options, with a set of MPP (Massive Parallel Processing) platforms added in as well, because many of the MPPs include the capacity to store schema-less objects internally using interpretable data, such as JSON objects, and also externally using flat files. The database vendor engine landscape has diversified, the reasons for which are not that important, but what is important is that users match their use cases to the correct database engine and vendor. Quite often what happens is that database tools are mixed up when organizations attempt to build a data warehouse using a relational database, or use a BigData platform to build a data warehouse, both of which can have some cost consequences in the long term.

COLUMNAR	KEY-VALUE	DOCUMENT-COLLECTION	GRAPH	MPPs & WAREHOUSES
Google BigTable	Memcached	CouchDB	Neo4j	Netezza
Hbase (Hadoop)	Redis	MongoDB	GlockDB	Yellowbrick
Cassandra	Tokyo Cabinet	SimpleDB	InfiniteGraph	Vertica
HyperTable	Dynamo	Lotus Domino	intGrid	Snowflake
Snowflake	Dynomite	Mnesia	orientDB	Redshift
	Riak		ravenDB	
	Project Voldemort		Giraph	
	scalaris			
	Redis			
	Oracle NoSQL			

Figure 7.6 NoSQL database vendors in recent years, with some MPP data warehouses added.

Note in Figure 7.6 that Snowflake is listed as both columnar and a warehouse, which is an interesting distinction to make, because Snowflake is popular, having been designed as a columnar database for warehousing that also allows for flexible datatypes (storing JSON objects), and can thus potentially function as a BigData data store as well. There are further categories of database models and storage tools; these all exist currently in AWS (Amazon Web Service), showing that modern database engines are specialized without attempting to be a magic box of tricks that does everything, such as Oracle Database attempted to do in recent years:

- **Relational**. Schema on read and write, referential integrity between primary and foreign keys guaranteeing no orphaned data and no duplication. Built for small scale read/write transactional databases.
- **Columnar**. Internal storage is built as physically separated columns as opposed to physically separated tables and rows.
- **Key-Value**. Schema-less, fast insertion, slow retrieval, high through-put of large data quantities.
- **Document Collection**. Indexed stored documents structured in a hierarchy where each index leads down the hierarchy to the next layer within the parent branch of the hierarchy. The result is a well-structured collection of documents where each node links to one parent and two or more children, with no connections outside of or across the hierarchy. A document collection database model is very similar to a pre-relational database model called a *hierarchical database model,* as shown in Figure 7.7 (repeated from Figure 1.2).

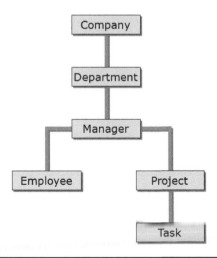

Figure 7.7   The pre-relational hierarchical database model.

- **Graph**. Very effective at finding a path through a multi connected network where each node can be connected to any other node. Applications include detecting credit card theft, identity theft, social network tracking, real-time BigData analytics, to rapidly find problems based on networking connections. So a graph database is also hierarchical, like a document collection hierarchy, except that linking between any

object across the hierarchy is allowed, regardless of hierarchical position, creating a form of pre-relational network database, or even an
object database. So a graph model can be well applied to a connectivity use case or function. A graph database model is very similar to
a pre-relational database model called a *network database model* as
shown in Figure 7.8 (repeated from Figure 1.3).

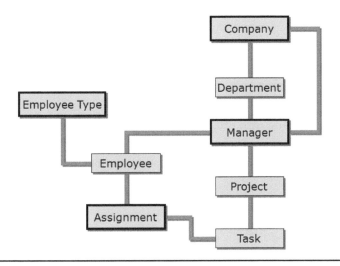

Figure 7.8   The pre-relational network database model.

- Three additional subset specialized database models currently provided by AWS are as follows,:
  o **In-Memory**. Very fast read and write access, but uses very expen-
    sive hardware to obtain that processing speed—this one is purely
    performance centric.
  o **Search**. Rapid indexed searching such as in data mining applica-
    tions that contain login or archived information; can potentially be
    used for data warehouse staging.
  o **Time-Series**. Information stored in time sequence and can poten-
    tially be used in data warehouse staging.
  o **Ledger**. Records a complete history of all changes to application
    data. This model is useful in systems where absolute accuracy and
    audit trail verification is required, such as for supply chain manage-
    ment, healthcare, and finance, and is likely an applicable model for
    the 3rd normal form data warehouse staging data vault model.

Open source and cloud database service database engines have evolved into specialized tools, with the result that many database vendor clients grow into the concurrent intellectual and financial investment of multiple database engines rather than a single all-encompassing one, and thus high software cost has partially been substituted for greater complexity and higher labor costs.

7.3 Four Main Types of BigData Modeling Architectures

The next thing to do is to attempt to break down, analyze, and understand the most significant approaches to BigData modeling. The most commonly used BigData architectures are columnar, key-value store, document collection, and graph.

7.3.1 Columnar BigData Modeling

There is not really much data modeling for a column-based database, because the tables are essentially denormalized star schemas, sometimes called *flattened tables* because they are join denormalized into single data mart equivalent tables. As for any BigData approach for data modeling, the modeling is in the entire ecosystem, where a column-based database simply stores data in columns as opposed to rows, and possibly even partitions by column (vertically) in addition to row (horizontally). Note that when a relational database creates an index, the index's most basic structure is a copy of the indexed fields plus an address back into the table, and given that a columnar database splits tables by column, those columns are quite similar to indexes, and therefore columnar databases do not have indexes because indexes are superfluous.

A column-based database stores data by column rather than row, which changes only the internal physical structure; the logical side of the database is the same with tables and views and variable datatypes to store unstructured JSON objects. ANSI standard SQL can still remain in use, making transition easier and thus more amenable to an existing market.

What column storage does do is cater to extremely large tables with many columns, typical of BigData database tables, and so it follows that this:

```
SELECT author, print_date FROM books;
```

will be far more efficient than this:

```
SELECT * FROM books;
```

Because the column-specific query reads two columns only, and the * syntax will force reading of an entire table that could have hundreds of columns, the less data that is read the faster a database becomes. The table accessed above is shown in Figure 7.9 where the flattened SALES, EDITIONS, and PUBLICATIONS tables as shown in Figure 7.4 are flattened further into a single table called BOOKS, which is typical for a BigData environment.

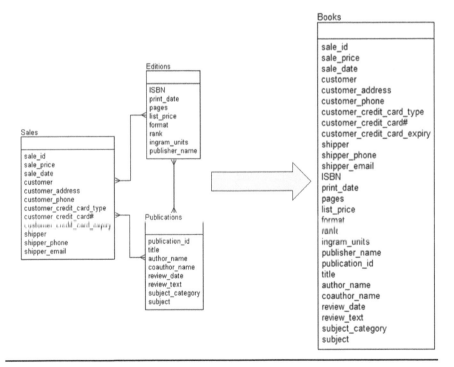

Figure 7.9   Denormalizing multiple functional datamarts into a single BigData table.

7.3.1.1 Demonstrating Row-Based Relational Database Architecture

Figure 7.10 shows a simple data set presented in row format.

ROWID	ISBN	AUTHOR	TITLE	GENRE	PRINT_DATE
1	1585670081	James Blish	Cities in Flight	Science Fiction	
2	345333926	Larry Niven	Ringworld		30-Nov-90
3	345336275	Isaac Azimov	Foundation	Science Fiction	31-Jul-86
4	345438353	James Blish	A Case of Conscience	Science Fiction	
5	553293362	Isaac Azimov	Second Foundation		
6	553278398	Isaac Azimov	Prelude to Foundation		
7	553293389	Isaac Azimov	Foundation's Edge		
8	553293370	Isaac Azimov	Foundation and Empire		

Figure 7.10 A visual representation of rows stored in a table.

Disk seeks are expensive operations in time, and in warehouses and BigData environments it is better to read lots of data that is contiguous (in the same place on disk), because it limits disk seek times (bouncing around the disk). Organizing data in rows that fit into contiguous blocks is better for tables where all the columns are selected, but not with large and wide fact tables where all columns are read. The text below shows a simple physical representation of row-stored data, where all the columns are grouped by and subsequently searched for with a ROWID:

```
ROWID,ISBN,AUTHOR,TITLE,GENRE,PRINTED
1:1585670081,James Blish,Cities in Flight,Science Fiction,
2:345333926,Larry Niven,Ringworld,,30-Nov-90
3:345336275,Isaac Azimov,Foundation,Science Fiction,31-Jul-86
4:345438353,James Blish,A Case of Conscience,Science Fiction,
5:553293362,Isaac Azimov,Second Foundation,,
6:553278398,Isaac Azimov,Prelude to Foundation,,
7:553293389,Isaac Azimov,Foundation's Edge,,
8:553293370,Isaac Azimov,Foundation and Empire,,
```

> A ROWID is a concept that described an internal disk identifier for a row physically located on disk, such as a block or set of contiguous or linked blocks.

So in Figure 7.10 and the text above, data is stored in rows. As data is added to the database, the row is assigned a unique row identifier, which is a logical or physical address on disk that represents where a disk seek would be able to locate the row in a hard disk scan process. The rows are assigned sequential identifiers that are added to each row's data as it is inserted.

The result is that: 1) row based is not efficient when pulling a small sub-set of columns from a wide table, and 2) row-based databases are not always efficient at querying a set-wide operation that pulls all rows from the same table. So in order to read smaller numbers of rows, indexes can be used to limit rows retrieved or target specific rows, but that results in two searches: one on the index and on one the table from the index. Also, partitioning and partition pruning is important as well, where small subsets of rows across an entire table can be retrieved based on a key identifying a subset partition of rows within a table.

Creating an index on the AUTHOR column from Figure 7.10 would look something like you see in Figure 7.11, which would then be used to link between index and table for each author, row by row, which for large num-bers of rows is very inefficient.

ROWID	AUTHOR	PRINT_DATE
1	James Blish	
2	Larry Niven	30-Nov-90
3	Isaac Azimov	31-Jul-86
4	James Blish	
5	Isaac Azimov	
6	Isaac Azimov	
7	Isaac Azimov	
8	Isaac Azimov	

Figure 7.11 An index is a subset of columns of the entire column set from a table.

A textual representation of the index shown in Figure 7.11 would look something like the sample as shown below.

```
1:James Blish
2:Larry Niven,30-Nov-90
3:Isaac Azimov,31-Jul-86
4:James Blish
5:Isaac Azimov
6:Isaac Azimov
7:Isaac Azimov
8:Isaac Azimov
```

7.3.1.2 Demonstrating Column-Based Data Warehouse Database Architecture

So index plus table makes for slow performance when reading too many rows, and thus a rearrangement of the following row format storage would store a table like this:

```
ROWID, ISBN, AUTHOR, TITLE, GENRE, PRINTED
1:1585670081,James Blish,Cities in Flight,Science Fiction,
2:345333926,Larry Niven,Ringworld,,30-Nov-90
3:345336275,Isaac Azimov,Foundation,Science Fiction,31-Jul-86
4:345438353,James Blish,A Case of Conscience,Science Fiction,
5:553293362,Isaac Azimov,Second Foundation,,
6:553278398,Isaac Azimov,Prelude to Foundation,,
7:553293389,Isaac Azimov,Foundation's Edge,,
8:553293370,Isaac Azimov,Foundation and Empire,,
```

into the below column-based storage with each column stored with a ROWID is shown below. So a column-based database with column format-ted storage would store a table like this:

```
James Blish:1,Larry Niven:2,James Blish:3,Isaac Azimov:4,
Isaac Azimov:5, Isaac Azimov:6, Isaac Azimov:7
30-Nov-90:1,31-Jul-86:2
```

Column-based storage can help to reduce the amount of physical disk space scanned. Note that possibilities for partitioning extend easily in col-umn-based databases, to include both horizontal partitioning (by row), as well as vertical partitioning (by column). In addition, options for partition pruning performance improvements increase in a column based architec-ture, which increases full table scans (full set searches) and further removes the need for indexing in column-based databases.

> In large-scale databases, it is all about how much data is read at a time, as opposed to relational transactional databases, which is all about reading and sharing small amounts of data very pre-cisely between many users.

So the efficiency of row based versus column based depends on the workload, where narrow tables and small row subsets are likely to be more effective with a row-based storage approach. For a column-based approach, wide tables and large set data queries are more likely to perform best. Retrieving data for large sets with a single disk read of a single seek or a single large contiguous set of blocks is desired, where bouncing around the disk with many separate disk seeks can have a poor effect on performance. Also, when adding data, column-based databases are more effective where not all rows have every column, and in reality column-based databases appear to clearly demonstrate many advantages in performance, despite the purist theory that dictates that the accuracy and integrity of row-based indexed performance should be better. In practice, and this has always been the case even in relational databases, the more data that is read for a query or added in an insertion, the more likely indexes will be ignored by database cost-based optimization.

Column-based databases provide better scope for sorting, given that sortable columns are physically grouped together, and there is also more opportunity for compression, because the same datatypes of data in columns are grouped together.

Finally, it is always very interesting to note that column-based database technology, both as a theoretical idea and a practical implementation, has been in use since the 1960s; it is nothing new in the form of databases called TAXIR back in 1969, TODS in 1975, and RAPID in 1976 and as with most database technology, quite often the ideas go back a long way into the past.

7.3.2 Key-Value Store Data Modeling

Key value data modeling is schema less, and thus the modeling aspect is largely defined within the key-value store as a set of key-value pairs, stored as duplications or iterations of the same key-value structure in a collection, also known as an *associative array*. Each element in the collection can contain a different group of fields for every row, thus using less space by not needing to create NULL entries, which also helps search speeds. The key-value approach is also closer to the object model than the relational database model, which is important because developers use object-oriented tools to build code, and it has long been a problem trying to create a mapping mechanism between objects and relations. Therefore, using a database that maps well to object-oriented development tools like Java helps to resolve the object-relational mapping mechanism more effectively.

> In BigData the modeling process is not in the data structures, but in the entire ecosystem. So key-value data stores can also be improved performance-wise using hardware solutions such as key sorting, in-memory stored data, and solid state disks.

Figure 7.12 shows a simplistic visualization of how a relational table can be re-architected into a key-value store table. Note the difference between Row1 and Row2, where Row2 contains a PRINTED key-value pair, and Row1 does not, because PRINTED does not exist for Row1; this is because the key-value store does not need to store the NULL value as the relational model would.

Key-value stores are very simple, perform well when partitioned physically by keys, are resilient to failure, allow high throughput in large databases such as warehouses or BigData databases, and their performance is consistent with scaling meaning that performance is consistent regardless of data store size. Key-value stores lack indexes and scanning capabilities, and so performing large complex queries including multiple table joins will perform very poorly.

Key-value stores can be useful for applications such as information about Twitter tweets, information about an Amazon item, or something like Priceline flight details. These are all applications where there is little connectivity between different functions. For example, different Twitter user data is not related to other users in that users should not be seeing each other's data, Amazon users do not get to see each other's book choices, flight details remain private.

7.3.2.1 JSON (JavaScript Object Notation)

It is useful to explain JSON by example in order to visually demonstrate what a key-value structure looks like. JSON is JavaScript Object Notation, which is a set of key-value pairs that represent both data values, as well as some of the semantics or meaning of that data. Thus JSON documents

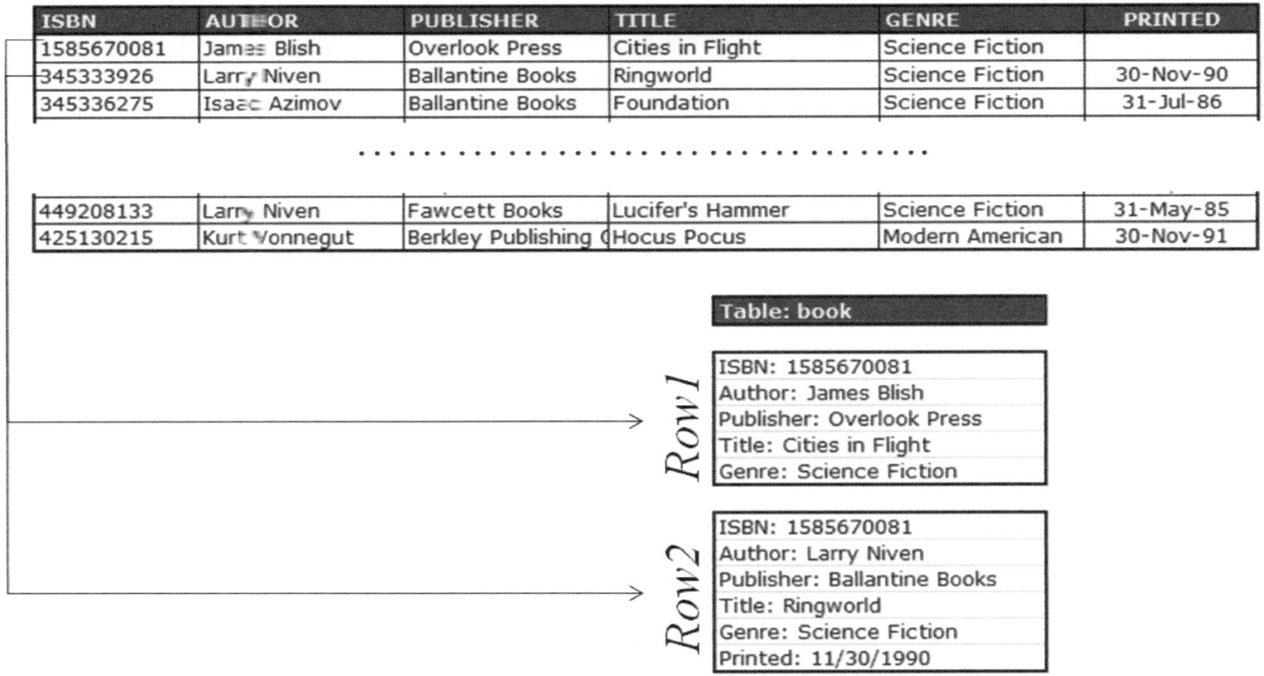

ISBN	AUTHOR	PUBLISHER	TITLE	GENRE	PRINTED
1585670081	James Blish	Overlook Press	Cities in Flight	Science Fiction	
345333926	Larry Niven	Ballantine Books	Ringworld	Science Fiction	30-Nov-90
345336275	Isaac Azimov	Ballantine Books	Foundation	Science Fiction	31-Jul-86
. . . .					
449208133	Larry Niven	Fawcett Books	Lucifer's Hammer	Science Fiction	31-May-85
425130215	Kurt Vonnegut	Berkley Publishing	Hocus Pocus	Modern American	30-Nov-91

Table: book

Row1
ISBN: 1585670081
Author: James Blish
Publisher: Overlook Press
Title: Cities in Flight
Genre: Science Fiction

Row2
ISBN: 1585670081
Author: Larry Niven
Publisher: Ballantine Books
Title: Ringworld
Genre: Science Fiction
Printed: 11/30/1990

Figure 7.12 Converting a relational table to a key-value store table.

can be built to contain both metadata (schema definitions) as well as data. So in a schema-less database, tables might contain JSON objects that are similar to Native XML databases of the past that might have contained an entire database inside a single XML document—a single JSON document contains a collection of one or more data elements. Individual elements consist of one or more name:value pairs, where rows can contain the same name-value pairs but do not have to, and thus each row entry (made up of a set of name-value pairs) does not have to have the same set of name-value pairs that all other rows in the same table do. Figure 7.13 repeats the simple books fact table star schema shown in Figure 7.2.

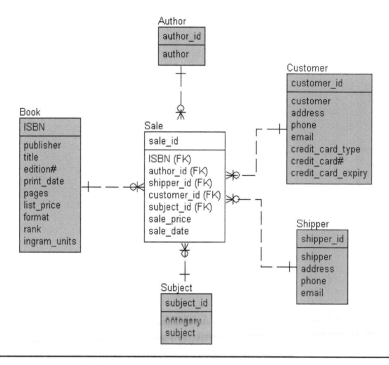

Figure 7.13 A simple fact table star schema structure.

Different tables in JSON format can be generated into separate files something like that shown below, as converted from the star schema as shown in Figure 7.13. This shows a simple JSON self-describing file containing the AUTHOR table data from Figure 7.13, and the JSON file is called author.json:

```
{
  "id": "1",
  "author": "Orson Scott Card"
},
{
  "id": "2",
  "author": "James Blish"
},
{
  "id": "3",
  "author": "Isaac Azimov"
},
{
  "id": "4",
  "author": "Larry Niven"
},
{
  "id": "5",
  "author": "Jerry Pournelle"
},
{
  "id": "6",
  "author": "William Shakespeare"
},
{
  "id": "7",
  "author": "Kurt Vonnegut"
}
```

Next is another JSON table representation of the Figure 7.13 SUBJECT table stored in a file called subject.json. Note that NULL values are not present in the JSON representation of the data:

```
{
  "id": "1",
  "author": "Orson Scott Card"
},
```

```
{
  "id":"1",
  "subject":"Non-Fiction"
},
{
  "id":"2",
  "parent":"1",
  "subject":"Self Help"
},
{
  "id":"3",
  "parent":"1",
  "subject":"Esoteric"
},
{
  "id":"4",
  "parent":"1",
  "subject":"Metaphysics"
},
{
  "id":"5",
  "parent":"1",
  "subject":"Computers"
},
{
  "id":"6",
  "subject":"Fiction"
},
{
  "id":"7",
  "parent":"6",
  "subject":"Science Fiction"
},
{
  "id":"8",
  "parent":"6",
  "subject":"Fantasy"
},
```

```
{
  "id":"9",
  "parent":"6",
  "subject":"Drama"
},
{
  "id":"10",
  "parent":"6",
  "subject":"Whodunnit"
},
{
  "id":"11",
  "parent":"6",
  "subject":"Suspense"
},
{
  "id":"12",
  "parent":"6",
  "subject":"Literature"
},
{
  "id":"13",
  "parent":"12",
  "subject":"Poetry"
},
{
  "id":"14",
  "parent":"12",
  "subject":"Victorian"
},
{
  "id":"15",
  "parent":"12",
  "subject":"Shakespearian"
},
{
  "id":"16",
  "parent":"12",
```

```
  "subject":"Modern American"
},
{
  "id":"17",
  "parent":"12",
  "subject":"19th Century American"
}
```

Next is another JSON table representation of the Figure 7.13 SUBJECT table stored in a file called subject.json (the three dots in the middle represent the collection objects or rows that are omitted from this sample):

```
{
  "isbn":"1585670081",
  "publisher":"Overlook Press",
  "title":"Cities in Flight",
  "edition#":"1",
  "pages":"590",
  "list_price":"34.5",
  "format":"Hardcover",
  "rank":"1000",
 "ingram_units":"100"
},

. . .

{
  "isbn":"345308999",
  "publisher":"Del Rey Bookss",
  "title":"Foundation",
  "edition#":"1",
  "print_date":"28-FEB-83",
  "list_price":"7.99",
  "rank":"1200",
 "ingram_units":"140"
}

. . .
```

Lastly, below is displayed an aggregate of data from Figure 7.13, containing AUTHOR and SUBJECT tables in addition to some other details. Note that the SUBJECTS collection contains more than one item as collections for Orson Scott Card and William Shakespeare, respectively, which demonstrates a collection within a collection. Also note how the details item sometimes contains an embedded address name-values pair, where the values are more than a single item.

This example is free-format embedded metadata JSON format in action, which is much more flexible than the rigid structure of a static pre-defined relational table structure—the relational structure is restricted by sequence, as well as the need for columns and datatypes. This file is called authorandsubject.json:

```
{
  "id": "1",
  "author": "Orson Scott Card",
  "subjects":
  [
    {
      "subject":"Science Fiction"
    },
    {
      "subject":"Critic"
    },
    {
      "subject":"Essayist"
    },
    {
      "subject":"Columnist"
    }
  ],
  "details":
  {
    "born":"August 4, 1951",
    "birth place":"Richland, Washington",
    "age":"67",
    "nationality":"American",
```

```
    "height":"6 foot 2 inches",
    "address":
    {
      "city":"Greensboro",
      "state":"North Carolina",
      "country":"United States"
    }
  }
},
{
  "id": "2",
  "author": "James Blish",
  "subjects":"Science Fiction"
},
{
  "id": "3",
  "author": "Isaac Azimov",
  "subjects":"Science Fiction"
},
{
  "id": "4",
  "author": "Larry Niven",
  "subjects":"Science Fiction"
  "details":
  {
    "full name":"Laurence van Cott Niven",
    "born":"April 30, 1938",
    "age":"81",
    "address":
    {
      "city":"Los Angeles",
      "state":"California",
      "country":"United States"
    }
  }
},
{
```

```
  "id": "5",
  "author": "Jerry Pournelle",
  "subjects":"Science Fiction"
},
{
  "id": "6",
  "author": "William Shakespeare",
  "subjects":
  [
    {
      "subject":"Shakesperian"
    },
    {
      "subject":"Sonnet"
    }
  ],
},
{
  "id": "7",
  "author": "Kurt Vonnegut",
  "subject":"Modern American"
}
```

7.3.3 Document Collection Data Modeling

A document collection database stores objects in a rigidly defined hierarchy. Document object databases are useful for social media postings, where each collection can contain many documents that have different fields across all the documents in the collection—and there is also no static metadata. Documents in document object databases are human readable, are flexible in their schemas and indexes, are stored in simplistic JSON-like documents, and allow for easy ad hoc queries and data aggregations. JSON documents in document collection databases are very similar to Native XML databases, except that JSON requires less information to denote than XML, and the result is JSON's more human readability. Next is a simple example of what a JSON document inside a document collection database might look like:

```
{
  id: 1,
  author: "Orson Scott Card",
  subjects: ["Science Fiction", "Critic", "Essayist",
"Columnist"],
  born:"August 4, 1951",
  birth place:"Richland, Washington",
  age":67,
  nationality:"American",
  height:"6 foot 2 inches",
  address: {city:"Greensboro", state:"North Carolina",
country:"United States"}
},

...

}
```

Document collection databases are useful for things like content management, mobile information, personalization, catalogs, retail and marketing, and user profiles. Existing document collection databases are hard to manage, hard to scale, hard to secure, and hard to backup—just like Native XML databases—because they are built within a strict hierarchical structure.

A document collection database contains a hierarchy of document collections inside collections, which creates a set of semi-structured data. The collection hierarchal structure can help determine inter-document relationships, but information inside each document can contain schema less data that does not have static structure, such as JSON documents or XML documents. The difference between a key-value store and a document collection database is as follows: in a key-value store things like JSON documents are not interpreted or processed directly by the database engine; however, in a document collection database the structure of the documents collection hierarchy helps to determine metadata and the semantic meaning of data.

Documents encapsulate and encode data using semantics contained with schema-less NoSQL objects (documents), such as XML, YAML, JSON, or BSON documents (or document objects). Documents can even be binary objects such as Microsoft Office documents like Word and Excel, or even PDFs. In relation to the database, contained objects are simply data and have no meaning to the database engine itself.

> Encapsulation refers to the concept of including processing or behavior with the object instances defined by a class. Encapsulation allows code and data to be packaged together, and data is defined within the attributes of an object. Processing or functionality is included within an object by use of methods defined for its defining class.

From a modeling perspective, document collection databases allow for CRUD access, which includes Creation (insertion of data), Read or query, Update, and Deletion. In addition, most object databases and NoSQL databases offer a built-in API (Application Programming Interface), which allows for direct access to one or more documents by direct key access and filtering based on content within a document. This even allows retrieval of parts of multiple documents, which contain schema-less but semantically meaningful data inside document objects, such as JSON and XML documents.

In a database engine such as MongoDB, there is an API allowing access and change to metadata, including document content and hierarchical position. In the past, relational database vendors added the ability to store schema-less objects such as JSON and XML documents inline within tables, plus they also provided the APIs to work with them. More specifically, Oracle and SQL Server provided storage of XML through text binary objects, as well as expression based API commands that could execute all CRUD operations on XML documents and their contents, all embedded within ANSI standard SQL commands as self-contained expression functions.

This embedding of XML documents into relational databases was an object-relational response to potential competition from object databases, which were ultimately less successful than their object-relational competitors in the commercial marketplace, and they also cannot compete with modern specialized document collection databases such as MongoDB. Figure 7.14 shows a super-simple sample of what a document collection database model might look like.

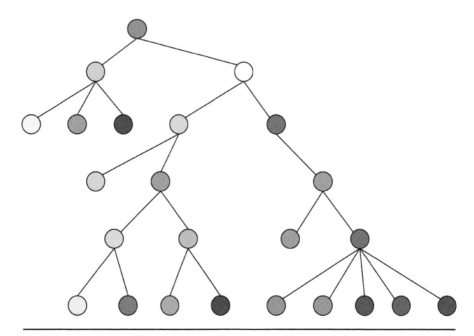

Figure 7.14 Visualizing a document-collection database looks like a hierarchy.

Figure 7.15 shows another very simple sample document collection data-base model, where labels contain collections of one or more labels or documents (links to documents in this case), structured in a clearly strictly controlled hierarchical structure.

For the next example, some changes are made to parts of the previous JSON samples in JSON pseudo code to add a few more layers, and this particular JSON object was validated using a free online tool called JSONLint (jsonlint.com):

```
{
        "id": 1,
        "author": "Orson Scott Card",
        "subjects": ["Science Fiction", "Critic", "Essayist",
"Columnist"],
        "details": {
                "born": "August 4, 1951",
                "birth place": "Richland, Washington",
                "age": 67,
```

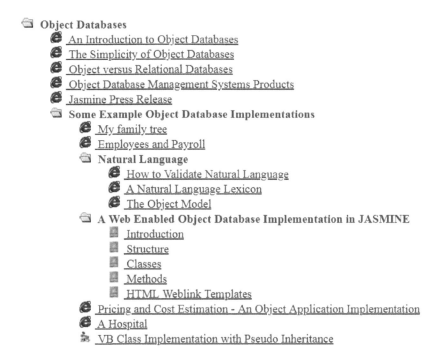

🗐 **Object Databases**
   📧 An Introduction to Object Databases
   📧 The Simplicity of Object Databases
   📧 Object versus Relational Databases
   📧 Object Database Management Systems Products
   📧 Jasmine Press Release
   🗐 **Some Example Object Database Implementations**
      📧 My family tree
      📧 Employees and Payroll
      🗐 **Natural Language**
         📧 How to Validate Natural Language
         📧 A Natural Language Lexicon
         📧 The Object Model
      🗐 **A Web Enabled Object Database Implementation in JASMINE**
         🖼 Introduction
         🖼 Structure
         🖼 Classes
         🖼 Methods
         🖼 HTML Weblink Templates
   📧 Pricing and Cost Estimation - An Object Application Implementation
   📧 A Hospital
   🗟 VB Class Implementation with Pseudo Inheritance

Figure 7.15   A simplistic visual representation of a document collection database model.

```
"nationality": "American",
"height": "6 foot 2 inches",
"address": {
        "city": "Greensboro",
        "state": "North Carolina",
        "country": "United States"

    }

  }

}
```

The above JSON script sample provides the basis for the hierarchical document collection structure as demonstrated in Figure 7.16, generated using the freebie version of a document collection database modeling tool called Hackolade® (hackolade.com), simply reverse engineering a JSON document into a visual representation showing a clear document-collection structural hierarchy.

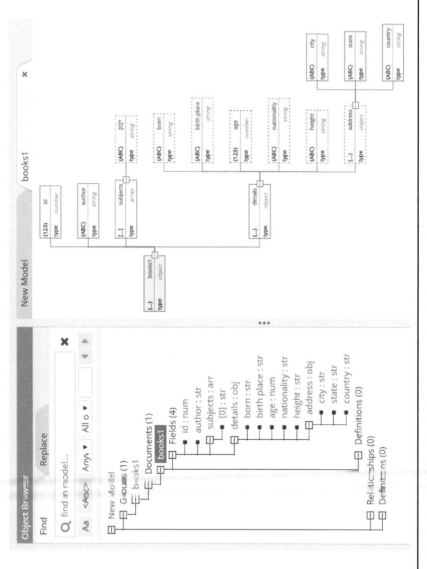

Figure 7.16 Visualizing a JSON object into a document collection model.

And below is a document containing a collection of multiple book documents:

```
[{
        "id": 1,
        "author": "Orson Scott Card",
        "subjects": ["Science Fiction", "Critic", "Essayist",
"Columnist"],
        "details": {
                "born": "August 4, 1951",
                "birth place": "Richland, Washington",
                "age": 67,
                "nationality": "American",
                "height": "6 foot 2 inches",
                "address": {
                        "city": "Greensboro",
                        "state": "North Carolina",
                        "country": "United States"
                }
        }
}, {
        "id": 6,
        "author": "William Shakespeare",
        "subjects": {
                "subject": "Shakesperian",
                "plays": ["Measure for Measure", "Romeo and
Juliet", "Hamlet"],
                "sonnets": {
                        "sonnet1": "FROM fairest creatures we
desire increase",
                        "sonnet2": "When forty winters shall
besiege thy brow",
                        "sonnet3": "Look in thy glass, and tell
the face thou viewest"
                }
        }
}]
```

7.3.4 Graph Data Modeling

Key-value stores create unstructured sets of key-value pairs. Document collection databases store collection hierarchies like hierarchical databases of
the past, where each object or document is only directly related to its child
collection documents or parent document. Graph databases are another
NoSQL accessed, schema-less key-value store that further develops the
hierarchical structure of the document collection model by adding inter-
connectivity across the hierarchy between any document, meaning that any
node can connect to any other node—similar to the network database of
the past model that suffered difficulties traversing a chain of connections.

Some application uses for graph databases include identity theft detection, fraud detection such as credit card theft, social media connections
marketing, internet of things analytics, telecommunications tracking, and
even automated product recommendations such as adverts appearing on
consumer computer screens as people search the internet. In effect, the
relationship and objects are structured so intensely that the data model
itself becomes the database, where all the data is defined by each relationship of each node with all the other nodes it is connected and related to—a
little like a neural network, a little like the way the brain is wired.

The graph database model consists of nodes, edges, and properties:

- **Node**. A node is a trackable object entity and is the equivalent of a
  row in a table in a relational database.
- **Edge**. Edges are the relationships or graphs between and connect-
  ing nodes, where edges represent the connections between nodes.
  There is always a start and an end node, and there can be multiple
  nodes from and to each node:
  - **Undirected Graph**. An edge that passes from one node to another.
  - **Directed Graph**. An edge that passes between two nodes in both
    directions.
- **Property**. A property is information or an attribute that is directly
  attached to or describing a node and stored as key-value pairs.

Graph databases are defined by their structure, where that structure or
metadata can be stored in a relational table in a relational database—but just
the metadata. On the other hand, a graph database's data is can be stored
in a key-value store or even a document collection database. A graph is flexible with data ingestion given that node addition simply adds new nodes and

edges and does not disturb existing structure. Performance is good because computing the shortest path between nodes is very effective, because a search follows the shortest path through the hierarchy of nodes and edges, without reading data that is irrelevant—searching is thus quite fast.

7.3.4.1 Types of Graph Data Models

Graph databases are useful to help in the analysis of metadata relationships between objects, as well as finding patterns in those relationships. Some different types of graph databases are as follows, type being different to application as described above:

- **Social Graph Model**. Connections between people are modeled.
- **Intent Graph Model**. Reasoning and motivation.
- **Consumption Graph Model**. Tracking individual customer consumption and making recommendations, which can also be called highly targeted marketing. For example, if one scans amazon.com for a specific type of guitar and does not make a purchase, then a rapidly updated graph database model might target that potential buyer the next time they open a browser that is or is even vaguely related to an online musical instrument vendor: targeted ads with the same type of guitar could be targeted at the user using search engine advertisements.
- **Interest Graph Model**. Mapping the interests of individual people and can be augmented by social graphs that connect individuals together, because the relationships between people can help to track their similar interests.
- **Mobile Graph Model**. Uses mobile cell phone data from telecommunications companies, including data from the internet, GPS tracking, IoI (Internet of Things), and more.
- **Other Graph Models**. Other types of specialized graph models include knowledge graphs, payment graphs, communication graphs, and others.

Figure 7.17 shows a very simple social graph model demonstrating a very small subset of connections between people that might be embedded somewhere within a social network; this model would make it highly efficient to scan across the network of nodes and edges to find a specific person and all the relationships, both with whom and in what nature,

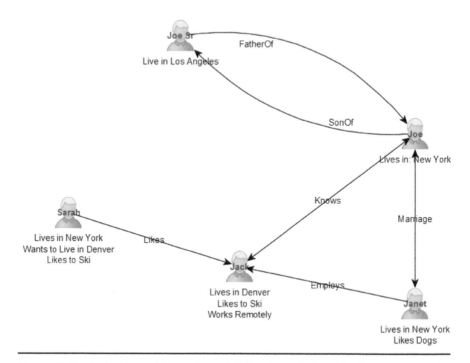

Figure 7.17   A simple social graph model showing relationships between people.

that an individual has with all other persons in that social network. Given that each node can have information attached about themselves, then the structure of the model itself can also be used to establish common attributes between people and even infer relationships between people.

Following on from Figure 7.17, in Figure 7.18, some or even all of the attributes can be moved from attributes into the model structure itself.

The graphs shown in Figure 7.17 and Figure 7.18 were drawn using a free graph database model editor called yEd™, which can be found at this URL: yworks.com

Graph databases can become very large and very complicated, such as the jumbled example shown in Figure 7.19, which is drawn automatically using a graph modeling and visualization tool called Gephi. The point made in Figure 7.19 is that the purpose of the graph database model is not to visualize the relationships for an entire database model, especially on a larger scale, but the intent is to model relationships between things mathematically. The result is a relationship-rich database model where changes and scans are more mathematically abstracted rather than

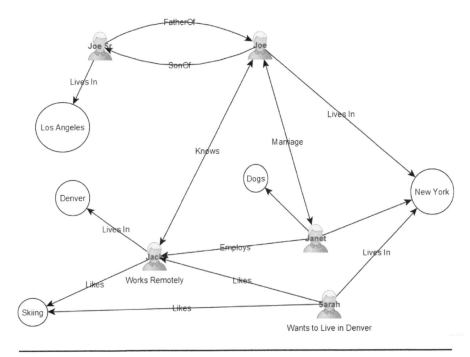

Figure 7.18 A social graph augmented by interests into a social interest graph.

Figure 7.19 Graphs are model data not metadata, but are used as mathematical abstractions.

literal, and visualizations could technically be drilled into in order to view a small section of a graph with the human eye, but it is more appropriate to approach a graph database model as an abstraction because of all the detail. This cycles back to the relational data model that implements simple mathematical sets of data, and the programmer reading and writing the database only really has to understand the sets, not necessarily the data.

7.4 Conclusion

This chapter covered:

- The Data Vault model for staging databases
- The Anchor model for staging databases
- Connecting the dots from relations and dimensions through to BigData
- BigData modeling terminology
- ACID versus BASE modeling
- NoSQL and Schema-less
- Columnar database modeling
- Key-value store modeling
- JSON (JavaScript Object Notation)
- 8Document collection data modeling
- Graph data modeling and types of graph data models

BigData is now a very important part of the information technology field, where a BigData environment is now much more than just a data model with tables and indexes, or a data warehouse fact-dimensional structure. A BigData database is an entire ecosystem of pieces put together that often service a specific type of use case or application function; however, a BigData model is simplistic in that the logical side of the modeling process has become partially redundant in comparison to the relational model.

This chapter has attempted to at least skim the surface of BigData database modeling by attempting to augment material from previous chapters, as opposed to rewriting the entire book and changing the book's existing layman's approach to relational data modeling as described in previous chapters; hopefully I have done it justice without being unfair to both either older or newer technology and approach to database modeling.

Index

#

1st normal form/1NF, 63–67, 93–97,
103, 149

2nd normal form/2NF, 63–67, 93,
96–99, 149, 150

3rd normal form/3NF, 63–67, 93,
98–103, 113, 150, 152, 166, 181,
182, 198–200, 203, 215

4th normal form/4NF, 63, 93, 100,
103–106, 150

5th normal form/5NF, 93, 100,
106–111, 150, 151, 154

A

ACID model, 210, 211
aggregate, 59, 229
aggregated query, 119, 127
analytics, 13, 206, 211, 214, 238
anchor model, 199, 203, 204, 242
anomaly, 82, 88, 103, 105, 107, 109,
112, 114
associative entity, 151, 202
associative table, 36

attribute, 27, 59, 79, 93, 161, 202,
204, 233, 238, 240,
auto counter, 16, 43, 60

B

balanced tree, 53
BASE model(ing), 210, 211, 242
basic query, 119
BCNF. *See* Boyce-Codd Normal Form
BigData, 2, 12–14, 59, 147, 149, 160,
168, 173, 195–198, 202–218,
222, 242
BigData database, 149, 211, 217,
242
BigData model(ing), 195, 198, 205,
206, 211, 216, 242
binary object, 10, 21, 20, 204, 208,
233
binary tree, 53
bitmap index, 54, 55
Boyce-Codd Normal Form (BCNF),
93, 100–103, 150—153
BTree index, 41, 53–56, 59

C

candidate key, 90, 93, 101–103, 150–153

Cartesian product, 130, 179, 180

class, 8, 161, 164, 165, 233

client-server database, 10, 11

cloud-based database, 12

cluster/clustered, 59

clustered index, 56, 59, 158

collection arrays, 21, 27, 28

column, 6, 16–24, 28–30, 39–53, 56–60, 64–67, 70–73, 83–85, 90–98, 101, 103, 107, 108, 112, 116, 120–122, 126–134, 137–139, 142, 143, 146, 150–152, 158–161, 185, 203, 216–221

Columnar BigData Modeling, 216

column-based database, 216, 220, 221

complex datatype, 21, 27, 28

composite index, 56, 57

composite key, 46, 50

composite query, 119, 137

compressed index, 57

constraint, 16, 19, 20, 21, 29, 30, 46, 47, 60, 142, 143

Consumption Graph Model, 239

cross join, 130, 134

crow's foot, 33

cyclic dependency, 92, 93, 106, 107, 150, 152, 154

D

data governance, 206

data lake, 208, 211

data mart, 7, 12, 59, 166, 175, 181, 182, 184, 199, 216

data science, 206, 211

data store, 13, 173, 206, 209–213, 222

data swamp, 208, 211

datatype, 16, 20–29, 60, 94, 137, 209, 213, 216, 221, 229

data vault hubs, 204

data vault model, 199–204, 215, 242

data vault satellite, 204

data warehouse, 11–13, 54, 57, 60, 114, 147–149, 158, 165–177, 181–187, 191–206, 210–215, 220, 242

data warehouse model(ing), 13, 165, 167, 169, 183, 195, 181, 198, 199

decision support database, 11, 171

decision support systems (DSS), 10, 11, 172

declarative programming, 115, 117

DELETE, 88, 119, 138, 139, 146, 184, 199

delete anomaly, 88

denormalization, 114, 147–150, 154–160, 167, 168, 209

denormalize(d), 105, 135, 149–151, 156, 159, 165, 174, 177–181, 191, 194, 206, 216

dependency, 9, 64, 67, 83, 84, 89–93, 96–99, 103–107, 143, 149–154, 165

dependent entity, 40

descending index, 56

determinant, 62, 89, 93, 101, 114, 150

dimensional database model, 174